Cambridge Elements ⁼

Elements in the Philosophy of Mathematics
Ediited by
Penelope Rush
University of Tasmania
Stewart Shapiro
The Ohio State University

MATHEMATICAL RIGOUR AND INFORMAL PROOF

Fenner Stanley Tanswell
Technische Universität Berlin

Shaftesbury Road, Cambridge CB2 8EA, United Kingdom

One Liberty Plaza, 20th Floor, New York, NY 10006, USA

477 Williamstown Road, Port Melbourne, VIC 3207, Australia

314–321, 3rd Floor, Plot 3, Splendor Forum, Jasola District Centre, New Delhi – 110025, India

103 Penang Road, #05–06/07, Visioncrest Commercial, Singapore 238467

Cambridge University Press is part of Cambridge University Press & Assessment, a department of the University of Cambridge.

We share the University's mission to contribute to society through the pursuit of education, learning and research at the highest international levels of excellence.

www.cambridge.org
Information on this title: www.cambridge.org/9781009494380

DOI: 10.1017/9781009325110

First published 2024

A catalogue record for this publication is available from the British Library.

ISBN 978-1-009-49438-0 Hardback
ISBN 978-1-009-32510-3 Paperback
ISSN 2399-2883 (online)
ISSN 2514-3808 (print)

Mathematical Rigour and Informal Proof

Elements in the Philosophy of Mathematics

DOI: 10.1017/9781009325110
First published online: March 2024

Fenner Stanley Tanswell
Technische Universität Berlin

Author for correspondence:
Fenner Stanley Tanswell, fenner.tanswell@gmail.com

Abstract: This Element looks at the contemporary debate on the nature of mathematical rigour and informal proofs as found in mathematical practice. The central argument is for rigour pluralism: that multiple different models of informal proof are good at accounting for different features and functions of the concept of rigour. To illustrate this pluralism, the Element surveys some of the main options in the literature: the "standard view" that rigour is just formal, logical rigour; the models of proofs as arguments and dialogues; the recipe model of proofs as guiding actions and activities; and the idea of mathematical rigour as an intellectual virtue. The strengths and weaknesses of each are assessed, thereby providing an accessible and empirically informed introduction to the key issues and ideas found in the current literature.

Keywords: mathematical rigour, informal proof, mathematical practice, formalisation, epistemology of mathematics

ISBNs: 9781009494380 (HB), 9781009325103 (PB), 9781009325110 (OC)
ISSNs: 2399-2883 (online), 2514-3808 (print)

Contents

1 Prologue: Three Proofs?

Before we begin with the philosophy, an Element about mathematics should start with some mathematics.

Proof 1: Sums of Odd Integers

Here is a classic proof by De Morgan (1838), updated into modern notation:[1]

Theorem: The sum of the first n odd positive integers, starting from one, is n^2.

Proof: *Let $P(n)$ be the statement "$\sum_{k=1}^{n}(2k-1) = n^2$".*

Since $\sum_{k=1}^{1}(2k-1) = 1 = 1^2$ we see $P(1)$ is true.

Assume $P(n)$ is true. Then

$$\sum_{k=1}^{n+1}(2k-1) = \sum_{k=1}^{n}(2k-1) + (2(n+1)-1) = n^2 + 2n + 1 = (n+1)^2.$$

Hence $P(n+1)$ is true.

Since $P(1)$ is true and $P(n+1)$ follows from $P(n)$ we conclude that $P(n)$ is true for all n by the principle of mathematical induction.

This proof is a typical rigorous proof, the sort students are given when they first learn about mathematical induction. In their study of mathematical rigour, Sangwin and Kinnear (2021) found this proof to be rated by far the most rigorous presentation of this result amongst a selection of different proof methods and styles. There are no errors and no gaps. This proof accordingly can be taken as a paradigm example of informal rigour.

Proof 2: Malfatti's Marble Problem

In contrast to the previous correct and rigorous proof, let us look at the history of a *failed* proof:[2] that of Malfatti's marble problem.[3] The problem is about how to cut three circular "pillars" out of a triangle while minimising the amount of marble wasted. Mathematically: within a given triangle, to find three non-overlapping

---

[1] The exact version I'm using here is by Sangwin (2023).
[2] A terminological note on the word "proof": one way of using "proof" is as a success term, meaning that "failed proof" is a *non sequitur*, or has to be read as "a failed *attempt* at a proof". A central theme of this Element is the philosophical complexity of separating correct, valid, or rigorous proofs from incorrect, invalid, or unrigorous ones. Therefore, I will use "proof" in the weaker sense of something like a "purported proof" or a "possible candidate for being a proof", meaning something created to be a proof, presented according to the norms of proof presentation, without obvious reasons for judging them invalid, and so on.
[3] This historical description primarily draws on Andreatta et al. (2011) and Lombardi (2022a).

circles with the greatest total area. This problem was named after Gianfrancesco Malfatti (1803), though it had also appeared earlier in Japan in the work of Chokuyen Naonobu Ajima and was studied for the special case of isosceles triangles by Jacob Bernoulli (see Andreatta et al. 2011).

In his article, Malfatti (1803) assumes that the solution to the marble problem is given by finding what are called the "Malfatti circles": the unique trio of circles inside a triangle that are tangent to one another and touch two sides of the triangle each (Figure 1).[4]

For Malfatti, the problem was to find a way to construct these circles for a given triangle. That is, he believed the area maximisation problem was solved via the circle construction problem. Malfatti himself worked on the latter problem to give an initial solution, and an elegant straightedge-and-compass solution was given by Steiner (1826). For a century, Malfatti's marble problem was considered settled.

However, it was shown by Lob and Richmond (1930) that the Malfatti circles do not always maximise the area, because in an equilateral triangle the "greedy" arrangement has a slightly larger area (see Figure 2). The greedy arrangement involves placing the largest possible circle first, then the largest possible one in the remaining space, then doing so once more.

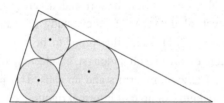

Figure 1 Malfatti circles.

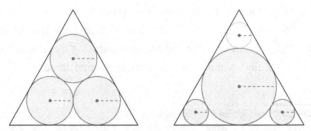

Figure 2 Malfatti circles and the "greedy" arrangement for an equilateral triangle.

---

[4] Images public domain, via Wikimedia Commons, created by user Personline.

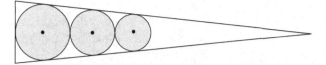

Figure 3 Optimal "greedy" arrangement for a long isosceles triangle.

Likewise, Eves (1965, pp. 245–7) noticed that for a long isosceles triangle it is better to stack three circles, as in Figure 3, than to use Malfatti's circles.

Amazingly, Zalgaller and Los' (1994) eventually showed that the Malfatti circles *never* have the maximum area, and Malfatti was simply mistaken. Zalgaller and Los' (1994) were themselves also attempting to make work by Los' four years earlier rigorous, work which they say "contained significant gaps" (p. 3163). Even then, their proof of the optimality of the greedy algorithm is incomplete, as argued by Lombardi (2022a). Their solution is based on enumerating the possible arrangements of circles and then excluding all but the greedy arrangement from being maximal, but the lemma that enumerates the possible arrangements is unproven. Furthermore, the trickiest case to exclude is tackled by numerical checking on sample points given in a table, rather than by a mathematical proof. The numbers being checked are also obtained by subtracting one decreasing function from another, but the numerical checking misses the fact that the total will not necessarily thereby be decreasing too.[5]

Only recently has Lombardi (2022a) closed these gaps and produced a fully rigorous proof of the maximal solution, which is the greedy arrangement and not the Malfatti circles. This history reveals four different failures of rigour: (1) the mistaken assumption smuggled in that one problem has the same solution to another; (2) making use of unproven lemmas; (3) using numerical methods that are not sufficient to establish the result; and (4) simple mathematical errors, like thinking a decreasing sequence subtracted from another is always decreasing. There are thus multiple seductive ways that mathematics can go wrong, even for such a seemingly simple problem. Nonetheless, this story also reveals some of the complexity of developing rigorous mathematics, ultimately culminating in a successful proof.

Proof 3: Hex Numbers

Finally, let us look at a tricky case. The following is one of my favourite proofs from the first volume of the *Proofs Without Words* series (Nelsen 1993, 2000, 2015) and is called "Sums of Hex Numbers are Cubes" (Nelsen 1993, p. 109), with the reader shown the first four hex numbers at the top to learn what they are, followed by the proof (Figure 4).

---

[5] Lombardi (2022b) details various other gaps and errors.

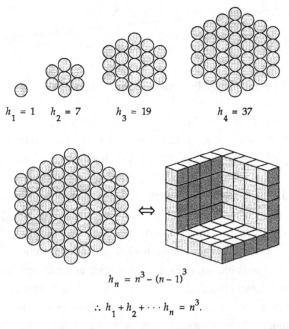

$$h_n = n^3 - (n-1)^3$$

$$\therefore\ h_1 + h_2 + \cdots h_n = n^3.$$

Figure 4 Nelsen's proof that sums of hex numbers are cubes. *Proof Without Words* © 1993 held by the American Mathematical Society.

One might call this a "proof by Gestalt shift", where the main idea involves a shift to seeing hex numbers in a different way, as the outer layer of a cube. While this is in my view a proof – if one understands it properly, one can see why the result must follow – it would be hard to argue that this is a *rigorous* proof. First of all, it never even gives an algebraic definition of what hex numbers are. Second, it implicitly contains an induction proof but does not make the key ingredients of an induction explicit. Third, the Gestalt shift is merely illustrated for the particular case of the fifth hex number, so understanding the inductive step requires us to fill in the reasoning of why it holds generally. Sufficient understanding and mathematical insight are enough to fill in these gaps, but there is no denying that they are gaps, and that the proof is gappy enough not to be rigorous by itself.

The questions we face, then, are: what is the difference between the three "proofs" we have seen? And what is mathematical rigour anyway?

2 Introduction

In this Element I will set out the range of answers that are available in contemporary philosophy of mathematics to the questions about rigour and informal proofs. Recent decades have seen a *practical turn* that shifts away from trying to answer philosophical questions about mathematics in the abstract alone and towards philosophical positions that are informed by the practices of mathematicians.[6] The idea is that mathematics, while being abstract and logical in its subject matter, is also a discipline shaped by human interests and values like any other, and that answers to questions about mathematical rigour are not independent of the activities involved in doing mathematics.

The concept of rigour can apply to many kinds of mathematical practices. The one that has interested philosophers the most, and which I shall focus on throughout, is the idea of *rigorous proof*. A rough first pass is that a rigorous proof is a detailed, logical proof that is free of errors and gaps. Another important application is *rigorous definition*, a definition that is precise enough to settle for all cases whether it applies or not.[7] The quest for *rigorous foundations* involves finding explicit axioms and inference rules to encode acceptable assumptions and reasoning for mathematics.[8] Furthermore, *rigorous areas of mathematics* are those where results and techniques are reliable, well-defined, and reproducible, with clear, agreed-upon inferential practices and foundations.[9] It is also common to see *mathematical rigour in physics* contrasting scrupulous and careful reasoning with more conjectural, empirical, or experimental approaches.[10]

Exploring the notion of rigour in all of these senses would be too much for such a short work, so my task will be to set out the contemporary debates on mathematical rigour and informal proofs. Broadly speaking, informal proofs are those proofs as written in actual mathematical practice, such as in journals, textbooks, lectures, seminars, classrooms, online forums, emails, scribbled on napkins, and so on. The central question is this: is there a single concept of rigour across these many mathematical contexts, and what is it?

2.1 The Purposes of Rigour

I think it is important to consider the purpose of having a concept of rigour and what it is being used for in the many contexts informal proofs might show up. In fact, the concept of mathematical rigour can be put to many different uses. This matches the idea that proofs themselves do not have a single purpose. Catarina Dutilh Novaes (2021, §11.4) surveys some of the main uses of proofs, listing

---

[6] Overviews of the state of the field of 'philosophy of mathematical practice(s)' have been given by Van Bendegem (2014), Löwe (2016), Carter (2019), and Hamami and Morris (2020).

[7] For more on definitions in mathematics, see Tappenden (2008), Cellucci (2018), Coumans (2021), and Coumans and Consoli (2023).

[8] See, for example, Maddy's (2017, 2019) careful work on the many possible purposes of set-theoretic foundations.

[9] For a case study of this going awry, see De Toffoli and Fontanari (2022, 2023) on the Italian school of algebraic geometry.

[10] See the discussion of the Jaffe–Quinn debate in Section 5.3.

verification, certification, persuasion, explanation, innovation, and systematisation. Likewise, we can list various functions that the concept of rigour is often said to be used for:

(1) **Soundness.** A rigorous proof protects us from errors and counterexamples. Historically, rigour was a driving force in the modernisation of mathematics. Concerns about infinite and infinitesimal quantities, especially in analysis, reached a peak in the nineteenth century with the appearance of mathematical 'monsters' such as the Weierstrass function, necessitating the "rigorisation of analysis" and ε-δ definitions.

(2) **Verification.** A rigorous proof verifies that a theorem is true.

(3) **Certainty.** Rigorous proofs are those that can be used to obtain mathematical knowledge. They can provide a high level of a priori justification, and absolute certainty in the truth of the theorem.

(4) **Body of Knowledge**. Rigorous proofs form a body of knowledge that other mathematicians can access and build on.

(5) **Social.** "Rigorous" is used as a label to identify which pieces of mathematics by other mathematicians are good and worth spending time on.

(6) **Demarcation.** The use of rigorous proofs is taken to be one of the main criteria that separates mathematics from other disciplines.[11]

(7) **Conviction**. A rigorous proof should convince a reasonable but tough audience of the truth of the theorem.

(8) **Peer Review.** Being rigorous is one of the standards for publishable mathematics. In assessing the work of other mathematicians in peer review, primarily for research journals, rigour is one of the main properties the proofs need to have.

This list is far from exhaustive but gives some of the main potential purposes of rigour.[12] Obviously, some of these purposes also link to purposes of *proof*, such as the idea that only a rigorous proof can truly verify a theorem. On the other hand, some purposes of proofs might be better achieved in a less rigorous fashion, for example, a proof might be more explanatory by providing a compelling intuitive idea than by rigorously going through all of the details. These purposes are debatable to varying degrees, so they can guide our discussion in the following section but cannot be immutable constraints on accounts of rigour. As we will see shortly, the plurality of purposes for rigour will connect to my proposal that we need to be *rigour pluralists*.

---

[11] This goal is notably defended by Auslander (2009).

[12] It also remains to be seen how successful mathematics is at meeting these functions. For example, the idea that mathematical proofs can produce certainty is a popular one but has been widely challenged (e.g. Kitcher 1984; Ernest 1998; De Toffoli 2021a).

2.2 Rigour in Principle and in Practice

One tricky feature of mathematical rigour is that it is used both descriptively and normatively. The *descriptive* use concerns when and why certain proofs are called "rigorous" in practice. The *normative* use concerns rigour as an ideal for mathematics, that is, that mathematics ought to be done in a way to meet the standards of rigour. These different uses raise different questions about rigour. The descriptive use of rigour poses an empirical question: which kinds of mathematics are actually described as "rigorous"? The normative use of rigour prompts two further questions. The first question is the *thoroughly normative* one: what standards or ideals should mathematics be held to? The second question is a *hybrid descriptive–normative* one: what standards do mathematicians *say* or *believe* they apply? It is possible for the answers to all three questions to come apart or coincide in any combination. Life would be simple if the descriptive use followed the normative; that the proofs described as rigorous were just the ones that meet the ideal standards, which are also just what mathematicians say they are. Alternatively, it could be that the answers all come apart; that the standards being applied are not the ones that mathematicians say they apply, which are also not the standards that ought to be used.

Of the three questions, only the normative one looks immediately philosophical and, even then, mathematicians might prefer to keep it for themselves to sort out. So, what role does philosophy play in untangling these various purposes and questions about rigour? The way I see the philosophers' job here is in giving accounts of mathematical rigour that enlighten and inform. The concept of rigour is multifaceted, unwieldy, and messy, so an account of rigour should try to unify and explain its main features. The list of purposes in the previous section is an example of this messiness: some of them are normative ideals, some of them are descriptive, and others can be read either way.

In the existing literature, the implicit approach to giving an account of rigour seems to be to find something like the "true essence" of mathematical rigour. This would seem to suppose that one concept is fulfilling all – or at least the most important – functions of rigour. A proponent of this approach would also likely say that they are most interested in the normative question of what the ideal standards of mathematics are. For them it would be better, but not essential, if this were to track mathematicians' practices and what they say those standards are. However, they must still be committed to at least approximating the descriptive features of mathematical practice because a theory predicting that all proofs described as rigorous are not actually rigorous would not be of much use in satisfying the functional roles of the concept. This leads to two connected challenges for an account of rigour to meet:

(1) **Functional adequacy**: to satisfy some or all of the main functions of the concept of rigour.

(2) **Descriptive adequacy**: to cohere with or approximate mathematical practices concerning rigour.

One purpose of this Element is to survey the existing positions and to argue that none of them provides an account of rigour that meets these conditions well enough to be the "true essence" of rigour.

2.3 Rigour Pluralism

Throughout this Element, I intend to adopt a novel position I shall call *rigour pluralism*. Instead of searching for a "true essence" of rigour and a unique correct account, I will take the different proposals in the literature as different *models of rigour*, in the sense of scientific modelling, and argue that all of these convey important insights. On this view, the existing accounts of mathematical rigour are seen as different theoretical models that each attempt to capture some combination of functions and descriptive and normative aspects of rigour. We will investigate which features of mathematical practice are incorporated into each model, and which are abstracted or idealised away. Unlike the "true essence" approach, however, these models will not be assessed as ultimately right or wrong. I believe that no such model is sufficient for all the purposes of the concept of rigour, nor are any of the models without merit. The rigour pluralist approach will be to assess the strengths and weaknesses of different models, evaluating which aspects of rigour they capture well, and which they do not.

A proponent of the "true essence" approach might try to object that the modelling approach is less plausible because its rigour is ultimately about logic, and that *a rigorous proof is a logical proof*. While I agree with this slogan, I do not believe the appeal to logic is definitive here. More basic than logicality, rigorous proof is about one way of doing *good* mathematics. On the modelling approach, we can say that formal logic can provide *models* of good mathematics and the mathematical reasoning found in proofs. The move to see this as also involving scientific modelling fits directly into the "logic as modelling" view put forward by Cook (2000, 2010), Shapiro (2014), and Kurji (2021).[13] Furthermore, it can be seen as exemplifying the approach of conceptual modelling proposed by Löwe and Müller (2011).

---

[13] The philosophy of logic has obvious import to questions about the philosophy of mathematics here, but has been surprisingly underutilised in debates about rigour. For example, the wider debates on logical pluralism (see Beall & Restall 2005; Cook 2010; Shapiro 2014; Russell 2019) and logical nihilism (see Franks 2015; Cotnoir 2018; Russell 2018; Kurji 2021) also show us that *logicality* is not a settled matter.

We will return to the idea of rigour pluralism across the coming sections to weigh how the various models of rigour and proof succeed and fail at capturing the features we are interested in. Furthermore, the selection of models is also meant to illustrate the pluralist position by showing that each of them models some aspects of rigour and informal proofs well, but that no account models all of the features well. A full defence of pluralism would take up more room than I have here, but I hope that considering the merits of a selection of models will illustrate the value of rigour pluralism as a viable and promising position for these debates.

2.4 The History of Rigour

My focus in this Element will be on setting out the contemporary research on mathematical rigour and informal proofs, so I will not be digging into the history of the development of mathematical rigour. Such a short treatment would not do it justice. Nonetheless, the history of mathematics is very important and, like any other concept, I hold that the concept of rigour cannot be fully understood without reference to the historical and social context from which it emerged. For a philosophical work that engages more explicitly with the historical development of rigour, see Burgess (2015, chs. 1 & 2). For a more recent part of the picture of proof and rigour, see Mackenzie (2004). A lot of excellent research in the history of mathematics is directly engaged with questions about the history of mathematical rigour and how conceptions of it have changed over time (e.g., Barany 2011, 2013; Haffner 2021; Cantù & Luciano 2021; De Toffoli & Fontanari 2022).

2.5 Outline

In the following sections, I will outline and evaluate a selection of models of rigour and informal proofs, grouped into four broad families. The first, in Section 3, is the most prominent and orthodox, sometimes called the "standard view": that *rigour is formality*. In Section 4, we will look at models of informal proofs and rigour that analyse proofs as arguments and dialogues. Section 5 will focus on the *recipe model of proofs*, where proofs are akin to recipes for mathematical activities. Finally, in Section 6, I will consider the idea of *rigour as an intellectual virtue* of the mathematician.

With this wide selection of models of rigour and informal proof I hope to illustrate the idea of rigour pluralism. These models are at different stages of development, with some long-established and others more recent, but I believe all of them are viable models of mathematical rigour. My claim is that trying to settle which amongst these is the ultimate correct account of rigour and proof is fruitless. Instead, each offers a different way of modelling important features of the messy concept of rigour that tangles together norms of logic and mathematical reasoning, real practices of mathematicians and their communities, and a complex history of development. The project of this Element is to consider the strengths and weakness of each family of models, and to reveal how between them they let us see the diverse features of mathematical rigour.

3 The Standard View: Rigour as Formality

3.1 Introduction

Our first model of mathematical rigour is often referred to as the 'standard view' because it is seen as the default position in modern discussions of mathematical rigour.[14] The standard view is, roughly, that rigour in mathematics should simply and straightforwardly be understood as *formal* rigour. The sense of formality in question is that of formal logic, so that a rigorous proof must be a logical derivation in some system of formal logic.[15] The standard view emerged alongside modern logic, pioneered by prominent mathematical logicians like Frege (1884), Hilbert (1899), and Whitehead and Russell (1910), as part of a quest to find the logical foundations of mathematics (see Ferreirós 2008). These foundations required a way to guarantee that every step in a proof is in accordance with the exact rules of logic. Before long, this had solidified into the dominant view among mathematicians and philosophers, exemplified most prominently by the Bourbaki group (see Hamami 2019; Barany 2020). In turn, this legacy has been inherited by the contemporary proponents of formal, computer-checkable mathematics, such as Hales (2008), Gonthier (2008), Wiedijk (2008), and Avigad (2021).

The obvious motivation for this view is that formal derivations are by definition gap-free and have precise and explicitly stated standards of correctness. So, it is safe to say that all formal derivations are rigorous. It is extremely tempting to claim that formality is also the *only* way to be rigorous. If a proof has gaps or relies on inferential moves that are not explicitly stated, then this can introduce assumptions that are not justified or reasoning that could lead to flawed conclusions. An example of this was seen in the story of Malfatti's marble problem in the Prologue, where both incorrect assumptions and unrigorous methods led to unrigorous proofs. Detlefsen (2009) summarised the motivation for the standard view succinctly:

---

[14] In Tanswell (2015) and Azzouni (2020) this class of views has also been called "derivationist". As will become clear, I actually think that calling it the "standard view" in the singular is misleading because it is really a family of overlapping views with important differences, something also pointed out by Burgess and De Toffoli (2022).

[15] In fact, what counts as formality is not so straightforward. Dutilh Novaes (2011) identifies many different ways that logic can be said to be formal.

> The reasoning behind this view is straightforward: (i) proper proofs are proofs that either are or can readily be made rigorous; (ii) proofs that are or can readily be made rigorous are formalizable; therefore (iii) all proper proofs are formalizable (Detlefsen 2009, p. 17).

In this section, we will start in Section 3.2 with a simplistic version of this view, which involves a process of filling in the gaps of informal proofs, noting that this does not stand up to scrutiny. Next, in Section 3.3, I will outline various desiderata for a more defensible version of the view. With these in hand, Sections 3.4, 3.5, and 3.6 will look at a range of more sophisticated versions of the standard view, specifically ones involving routine translations, *in principle* formalisability, and derivation-indication. Section 3.7 will then give a long list of criticisms of the standard view. Finally, in Section 3.8 I will make the case that the standard view is not a correct account of mathematical rigour by itself, but that it is a powerful family of *models* of informal proof and mathematical rigour.

3.2 Filling in the Gaps

While the idea that rigour reduces to formality can be useful as a normative ideal, the standard view needs to offer more in order to successfully describe how people judge rigour. Most proofs produced by mathematicians are not formal, and it would be an odd result for something called the "standard view" to predict that almost no mathematics is ever rigorous. The standard view must therefore include another component that explains how informal proofs can nonetheless be rigorous in some sense. This can be approached in many different ways, but the common thread between them is the idea that informal proofs can be rigorous by corresponding to formal proofs, even if they themselves aren't formal proofs. In this way, formality can still be the gold standard for rigour, but informal proofs can meet this standard indirectly.

What the correspondence should amount to in order to identify rigorous informal proofs varies for different proposals. The simplest version of this idea is that informal proofs *abbreviate* their formal counterparts, meaning that simple, straightforward steps are left out from informal proofs, but could be restored by a process of *filling in the gaps*. Especially for simple proofs, this idea is very appealing because it explains why linking informal proofs to formal ones still maintains rigour. The reason is that the main steps are all still present, and the "missing steps" are actually just the easy logical moves that are too obvious to need stating. The informal proof is rigorous despite the gaps because any mathematician could easily supply the steps that have been left out.

However, the abbreviation approach glosses over many of the important details. For example, the steps that *are* given in informal proofs are also typically not in a formal language, so they would also need to be seen as abbreviations of formulas, which leads to the question of how exactly they should be translated. Informal proofs also don't flag which formal system is being used in the first place, and there are many, many options. Translating informal sentences into formal ones is not as straightforward as the "filling in the gaps" idea would make it sound, as can be attested by anyone who has ever attempted it. Furthermore, the abbreviation approach would also be less clear for more advanced mathematics, where the missing steps may be less obvious. Therefore, there are further complexities that the standard view needs to address.

3.3 Aims for the Standard View

Before we get deeper into possible ways of filling out the standard view, let's discuss what it should be aiming to achieve. In some of my previous work I have given various desiderata that the standard view might aim to meet (Tanswell 2015, sect. 2). Let us briefly survey these.

To begin, the main idea behind the standard view is to explain rigorous informal proofs:

> **(Rigour)** To give an account of how informal proofs are (or can be said to be) rigorous through their connection to formal proofs.

Furthermore, the account should be of practical use, in that it would ideally provide insight into which proofs do not live up to the criteria it establishes:

> **(Correctness)** To distinguish correct informal proofs from incorrect ones, that is, the correspondence should only link the informal proofs that are correct to the justifying formal proofs.

Rigour and correctness are closely connected. A rigorous proof will also be a correct one, and so specifying criteria for when a proof is rigorous will also specify a class of correct proofs. Conversely, one might think that there are correct proofs that are not rigorous, such as by skipping too many details while getting the overall ideas right, as in the sum of hex numbers proof that we saw in the Prologue. This class of proofs will have gaps but not errors, as correct proofs cannot contain errors.[16] One could, alternatively, argue that this class doesn't, strictly speaking, exist at all, that all proofs worthy of the name must be rigorous. In that case, there would be only two categories: correct, rigorous proofs, and

---

[16] Even this might be too strong for actual practice. In joint work with Joshua Habgood-Coote (2023), we consider the enormous proof of the *Classification of Finite Simple Groups*. In this case, the mathematicians seemingly accept the proof despite believing it will inevitably contain some errors due to its size, because they are convinced that these errors will be so-called local errors that could be fixed without too much effort, and which do not affect the correctness of the theorem overall.

failed proofs. This would amount to rejecting the proposed proof of the sum of hex numbers. (Maybe one could demote it to some intermediate thing, like a "proof sketch" or "proof idea".) Ideally, then, if the standard view is appealing to formal proofs to identify gaps and errors, it should provide guidance on how to separate correct and rigorous proofs from those which are not.

To articulate the standard view properly requires one to address the details of how a specific informal proof will link to a formal proof that explains its rigour. That is:

> **(Content)** To show how the content of an informal proof determines the structure of the formal proof(s) it corresponds to.

We will see in the following sections that different versions of the standard view take quite substantially different approaches to this task.

A particular difficulty that needs to be addressed by the standard view concerns informal techniques:

> **(Techniques)** To provide an explanation of apparently *inherently* informal techniques.

The most obvious of these would be to set out what is to be said about diagrams in proofs. There are multiple options for this, ranging from denying that diagrams can play an essential role in proofs at all, to explaining which diagrams are amenable to formalisation and how (see Brown 1999, ch. 3; De Toffoli 2023).

Finally, since the standard view is also attempting to give a descriptive account of how mathematicians judge rigour in practice, another aim they have is to account for the mechanism by which mathematicians *agree* on the rigour and correctness of informal proofs:

> **(Agreement)** To explain how, in practice, mathematicians manage to converge and agree on the rigour and correctness of informal proofs.

It is commonly taken as one of the virtues of the standard view that it would help to explain agreement among mathematicians. For example, Azzouni says, "[M]athematicians have a way of agreeing about proof that is virtually unique (agreement of any sort among humans is always a surprise, and always has to be explained somehow), and the explanation of this surely is that some sort of recognition of mechanical procedures is involved." (2004, p. 103).

However, recent empirical work has shown that mathematicians do sometimes disagree on what counts as a valid proof (Weber 2008; Inglis & Alcock 2012; Weber & Czocher 2019) and what counts as a gap or error in a proof (Inglis et al. 2013; Davies et al. 2021). This does not mean there is no agreement to explain; one notable finding from these articles is the importance of the context of the proof for evaluating its validity. The disagreement was also elicited by asking about difficult cases like diagrammatic proofs and computer proofs. So, by keeping the context fixed and choosing less borderline cases, there might still be higher agreement among mathematicians than researchers in other fields. One might also posit that there is something like long-term convergence on agreement, so that even if there can be disagreement about validity about some step or type of proof, over the long term mathematicians will converge on agreement. Of course, these are also empirical claims that can and should be tested.

In Section 2.1, I gave some of the purposes of having a concept of rigour at all, but it is noteworthy that this was not the same as the ambitions of the standard view. The standard view seems to be interested primarily in a subset of the broader uses of the concept, most obviously **Soundness** and **Verification**, though **Agreement** links to the social side of mathematics. In general, the explanation for this is that the standard view leans more towards the normative question of how mathematical theorems ought to be fully justified rather than the descriptive claim of mathematical justification in practice.

By setting out these aims for the standard view, we can judge individual components of the various proposals against their aims. For example, the simple "filling in the gaps" abbreviation model we already saw has proposals to answer **Rigour**, **Correctness**, and **Agreement**. However, we found the story for **Content** to be lacking in important details, and the answer to **Techniques** would likely need to reject anything, like diagrams, that cannot undergo the "filling in the gaps" process easily.

With a number of possible aims for the standard view, and a selection of options for what it might mean for informal proofs to correspond to formal ones, it now becomes clear that there is not really one standard view, but instead a family of standard views which share a commitment to the general idea that formal proofs explain which informal proofs are rigorous. In Sections 3.4, 3.5, and 3.6, I will survey three of the most prominent proposed options in more detail, and likewise evaluate them against the aims I have just considered.

3.4 Hamami's Routine Translations

Let us begin with the version of the standard view set out by Hamami (2019). Hamami claims that he is giving an exposition of the standard view as understood by most mathematicians and following the ideas of Saunders Mac Lane (1986) and the collective Bourbaki (1968) group.[17] For example, he quotes them as already defending some version of the standard view:

---

[17] For a discussion of the social dynamics of the Bourbaki group, see Barany (2020).

> A Mathematical proof is rigorous when it is (or could be) written out in the first order predicate language $L(\in)$ as a sequence of inferences from the axioms ZFC, each inference made according to one of the stated rules. ... To be sure, practically no one actually bothers to write out such formal proofs. In practice, a proof is a sketch, in sufficient detail to make possible a routine translation of this sketch into a formal proof. (Mac Lane 1986, p. 377)

> In practice, the mathematician who wishes to satisfy himself of the perfect correctness or "rigour" of a proof or a theory ... is content to bring the exposition to a point where his experience and mathematical flair tell him that translation into formal language would be no more than an exercise of patience (though doubtless a very tedious one). (Bourbaki 1968, p. 8)

Hamami describes how the standard view will have a normative and a descriptive component: the normative component will give the ideal of how a proof ought to be rigorous, while the descriptive component will pick out how judgements of rigour are actually made in practice. He argues that the condition that an informal proof should be "routinely translatable" into a formal proof provides a useful middle ground between these normative and descriptive parts. The idea is that routine translatability is a weak enough condition that proofs can meet it in practice, but nonetheless maintains the strong connection to the ideal of formal derivations. His proposal is that advocates of the standard view have an implicit conception of the mechanism for judging rigour, with reasons for thinking they will succeed in identifying when a proof conforms to the normative standard. The "conformity thesis" is Hamami's claim that every proof that is "descriptively" rigorous in practice also satisfies the normative ideal of formal rigour. In other words: the practice of rigour conforms to the ideal via an implicitly understood mechanism of formalisability.

Hamami's primary contribution is to give specifications of what the descriptive and normative accounts of rigour are for his version of the standard view,[18] and how they conform to one another. Let us take these in turn.

For the descriptive account, the general idea that Hamami proposes is that informal proofs involve sequences of "higher-level" inference patterns. These kinds of inferences are acquired as one learns mathematics. One begins with basic knowledge of mathematical statements and simple, obvious inferential moves, then proceeds to cumulatively gain knowledge by proving more things, and recognising more complicated higher-level inferences as acceptable by

---

[18] Hamami claims to be merely explicating the standard view as it is commonly held by mathematicians and filling out the details implicit in the works of Bourbaki and Mac Lane. I don't think this gives credit to the substantial additional ideas he brings to this debate.

verifying that they merely abbreviate some longer-established pattern of inferences.[19]

For the normative account, Hamami attempts to set out what a "routine translation" is, and to give a precise insight into how it will proceed. His view is that the routine translation is best understood as composed of three stages. The first stage takes an informal proof and fills in details so that the inferences use higher-level inference rules. The second stage unpacks those higher-level inference rules, fully breaking them down into the more basic inferences that they abbreviate. The third stage takes the sequence of basic inferences and formalises it into some formal system. Importantly, Hamami claims that this procedure is routine in the sense that it is algorithmic, mechanical, and automatic.

Finally, the argument for the conformity thesis uses the central role of higher-level inferences in both the descriptive and normative parts: Hamami's idea is that a descriptively rigorous proof will be made up of higher-level inferential moves, for which the routine translation will succeed, thereby reaching the normative ideal.

In terms of the aims of the account, Hamami's version of the standard view is clearly more sophisticated than the original "filling in the gaps" account. While he is still addressing **Rigour** and **Correctness**, the detailed description of the routine translation he gives is also addressing **Content**. Furthermore, the idea that mathematicians implicitly recognise the mechanism by which rigour is judged is intended to address **Agreement**, because the mechanism is, presumably, shared by mathematicians who are able to make the relevant judgements. The question of **Techniques** is less straightforward because it is not obvious that Hamami's account will apply and he does not explain how to deal with cases such as diagrammatic proofs. The descriptive account could potentially be the same: that one builds up a toolbox of acceptable diagrammatic inferences cumulatively. However, one quick objection is that this assumes that the acceptable inferences always come from this kind of process, and do not rely on previously untested inferences that take advantage of visual elements of the diagram, rather than being made up of smaller inferences.

3.5 *In Principle* Formalisability

Another version of the standard view is to think that rigorous informal proofs are those that would be formalisable *in principle*. That is, rather than thinking

---

[19] This descriptive account is similar to that given by Tatton-Brown (2023) who also thinks that mathematical learning is cumulative and thereby allows us to recognise more substantial mathematical inferences as rigorous, while still having those inferences ultimately "deductively grounded" in formal correctness.

there is a routine translation from a rigorous informal proof to a formal derivation, they instead rely on the theoretical possibility of such a translation. Prominent proponents of this kind of approach include Steiner (1975) and Burgess (2015).

Starting with Burgess, he builds on two general ideas about rigorous proof. The first is that: "A proof is what convinces a reasonable person; a rigorous proof is what convinces [even] an unreasonable person" (Burgess 2015, p. 91).[20] The second idea is that rigorous informal proofs are not about giving an abbreviated version of a formal proof, but instead are primarily about convincing other mathematicians that such a proof exists. Burgess refers to this principle from Hyman Bass, who says:

> The notion of mathematical proof is a precise theoretical construct, but it is quite formal, rule bound, and ponderous. Mathematicians typically do not produce such formal proofs, but rather convince expert colleagues essentially that such a proof exists, the presumption being that the conviction carries the belief that under duress and with sufficient time such a proof could be supplied by the proponent. (Bass 2003, p. 770)

Burgess summarises this in slogan form: "A proof is what convinces mathematicians that a formal proof exists" (Burgess 2015, p. 91). However, this is not adequate by itself because it is relevant *how* the conviction comes about. Being convinced can happen in numerous ways, such as through expert testimony or brainwashing. Even an unreasonable person might be convinced for the wrong reasons – given their unreasonableness, we might expect this even more – and certainly expert testimony can convince people of the existence of formal proofs. What Burgess is after is that the convincing isn't of this defective sort; that the convincing happens *in the right way*. He tentatively suggests that the right way for this conviction to come about is because the steps supplied show *enough* of the formal proof: "What rigor requires is that each new result should be obtained from earlier results by presenting enough deductive steps to produce conviction that a full breakdown into obvious deductive steps would in principle be possible" (Burgess 2015, p. 97).

In his review of Burgess's book, Pettigrew (2016) responds that it isn't about supplying enough steps, but about supplying the right steps. He observes that an advanced mathematician might only need to see a single trivial step of a very difficult proof to convince themselves that a formal proof exists, in virtue of their ability to come up with proofs, but that cannot

---

[20] Burgess ascribes this idea to Mark Kac. I've not managed to trace a direct quotation, other than in his obituary by Thompson (1986).

be the relevant sense of the "right way" to bring about conviction, because only supplying a trivial step does not make for a rigorous proof. Pettigrew proposes that what is missing from Burgess's account is a distinction between *ingenious* and *routine steps*. A proof should display all of the ingenious steps and thereby convince its audience of the existence of a formal proof: "A rigorous proof is one that convinces its audience that there exists a formally rigorous proof by providing those steps in the formally rigorous proof that it is not simply routine to provide" (Pettigrew 2016, pp. 132–3). The idea is that the routine steps are those that one can reasonably expect another mathematician to come up with for themselves, while ingenious steps must be given. Therefore, to convince other mathematicians of the existence of a formal proof, one needs to supply those ingenious steps, but may take the routine steps for granted.

A similar line of thought is present in Steiner's (1975) account of mathematical knowledge. He thinks that one can gain mathematical knowledge from a proof only if that proof is in principle formalisable. To fill out what "in principle" means he deploys the thought experiment of being able to produce a formal proof with the assistance of a hypothetical logician helper. Most mathematicians don't know enough formal logic to produce formal proofs, so it cannot be expected that they themselves can produce formal equivalents of their proofs. Steiner solves this by imagining what would happen if they were paired with a logician who could produce formal proofs. The logician would be able to handle the logic itself and the details of the routine steps, while the mathematician must supply the ingenious and creative parts of the mathematical reasoning. If, in the hypothetical, the two of them could produce a formal derivation together, then the informal proof would be sufficient to establish the mathematician's knowledge all along.

The *in principle* formalisability approach is clear with regard to **Rigour** but underspecified with respect to **Correctness**. After all, it is not obvious that supplying enough (or enough ingenious) steps of a proof is sufficient to guarantee its formalisability, nor is it clear that the hypothetical logician can really underpin an account of correct proofs. The *in principle* account seems to bypass the demand of **Content** altogether because it does not want to specify at all what an informal proof's corresponding formal proof is, let alone how the two are linked. For **Techniques**, this account rejects any proof techniques that are *inherently* informal, since they couldn't be formalised even in principle. For **Agreement**, a story is needed of how mathematicians converge on which proofs are formalisable *in principle*, though the suggestions of Burgess and Pettigrew provide an outline of how this could go.

3.6 The Derivation-Indicator View

One of the most influential proposals for making informal rigour dependent on formal proofs comes from the earlier work of Jody Azzouni (2004) on his *derivation-indicator* view.[21] We have seen the *routine translations* view try to specify how formal proofs correspond to a given informal proof, and the *in principle formalisability* view that informal proofs only need to be formalisable in principle. In contrast, the derivation-indicator view is that informal proofs do *indicate* corresponding derivations, but without the mathematicians needing to know how that correspondence works. These indicated derivations explain things like **Rigour**, **Correctness**, and especially **Agreement**, but do not need to be known to the mathematicians, nor are they fixed to a particular formalism.

The overall idea is that formal derivations are implicit in informal proofs, in a way that secures mathematical rigour because those derivations are mechanically checkable, which indirectly secures the informal proofs too.

> I take a proof to *indicate* an 'underlying' derivation ... Since (a) derivations are (in principle) mechanically checkable, and since (b) the algorithmic systems that codify which rules may be applied to produce derivations in a given system are (implicitly or, often nowadays, explicitly) recognized by mathematicians, it follows that if proofs really are devices mathematicians use to convince one another of one or another mechanically-checkable derivation, this suffices to explain why mathematicians are so good at agreeing with one another on whether some proof convincingly establishes a theorem. (Azzouni 2004, p. 84)

Mathematicians can agree on rigorous and correct proofs because they are implicitly sensitive to which informal proofs indicate formally valid, mechanically recognisable counterparts. Nonetheless, this doesn't require them to actually know what those indicated derivations are, which explains how mathematics could function in this way despite the long history of mathematics before the invention of formal proofs and despite the many mathematicians who are not able to produce formal proofs.

The proposal that the formal derivations are implicit and not necessarily known by the mathematicians themselves works in part because the derivations Azzouni has in mind are not fixed to a single formal system. Instead, they can be found across a whole family of algorithmic systems (with some technical caveats that we do not need to explore here). Mathematicians are not bound to some particular formalism, so neither are the derivations that underlie proofs.

---

[21] In more recent work, Azzouni (2020) has moved away from the derivation-indicator view towards the *algorithmic device* view of informal proofs. While this has some familial relationship to the derivation-indicator view, it also has some substantial differences that mean it explicitly no longer falls under the label of the "standard view".

Furthermore, new techniques can lead to needing the resources of different formal systems, and Azzouni sees mathematicians as flexible and free to move to new formal systems that can accommodate their needs: "On the derivation-indicator view of mathematical practice, the mathematician is seen instead as gracefully sprinting up and down algorithmic systems, many of which he or she invents for the first time" (Azzouni 2004, p. 103).

This means that informal proofs that make use of more meta-level reasoning are happening in a higher-level system that can handle them. Azzouni's example is using a "proof by symmetry", where just one of several cases is proven in detail and the rest are argued to follow symmetrically. He also takes this to allow the flexibility for there to be algorithmic systems that are indicated by diagrammatic reasoning, allowing for an answer to **Techniques**.

In other papers, Azzouni (2005, 2009) develops a novel account of "inference packages", which are "psychologically-bundled ways of phenomenologically exploring the effect of several assumptions at once without explicit recognition of what those assumptions are" (Azzouni 2005, p. 9). These work like cognitive black boxes which allow us to carry out mathematical manipulations without having to be able to introspectively know the underlying formal justification, or even to recognise which assumptions are being manipulated. That mathematicians often use inference packages to think about mathematics adds to the account by explaining how **Techniques** can seem so inherently informal and compelling while still indicating underlying derivations. Furthermore, it fills out how indicated derivations might secure **Agreement** among mathematicians despite them not knowing the exact derivations themselves.

Overall, Azzouni's derivation-indicator view does well at accounting for **Rigour** and **Correctness**, using the indicated family of derivations. For **Agreement**, mathematicians are meant to agree about validity because their judgements are tracking the implicit, indicated derivation. Meanwhile, by not needing mathematicians to be aware of which derivation is indicated, the account can address apparently inherently informal **Techniques** and not rely on the mathematicians knowing substantial formal logic, which is uncommon even now and was impossible prior to the relatively recent development of modern logic. One thing that is left somewhat underspecified is **Content**: the indicated derivations are meant to provide the ultimate source of justification for the informal proofs, but it is not clear how they do so or what the "indication" relation amounts to.

3.7 Criticisms of the Standard View

So far, we have been assessing the merits of the various versions of the standard view by the criteria from Section 3.3. However, this has taken for granted that the views broadly succeed in the first place. This is far from clear. One of the major contributions of the practical turn in the philosophy of mathematics has been to challenge the standard view with a wide selection of criticisms. In this section, I will survey some of the most prominent ones and add some more of my own. We won't have space to go into much depth, but the reader can follow the references for further discussion.

3.7.1 No Formal System

The first objection to the standard view is the absence of a specific formal system under discussion. Different systems will have different things they can prove and different ways of proving them, so what system underlies the rigour of informal proofs is far from an idle question. If the inferences found in an informal proof are warranted by one formal system but not by another, what is the status of that informal proof? This question applies at several levels. First, one might ask what underlying logic is being used. The default assumption would be classical logic, though the constructivists and proponents of other alternative logics would reject this. Even within classical logic, one must settle on using first-order logic, some higher-order logic, or something in between. One must decide about the acceptability of infinitary proofs.[22] At the technical level, these choices will matter as to what can be formalised and how. Beyond the logic, one must settle on which axioms are used. Again, the default would probably be those of ZFC set theory, which itself can be supplemented with all kinds of extra axioms, but there are alternative proposals for foundations of mathematics too, such as through category theory or homotopy-type theory. Again, these would affect what could be formalised.

Multiple formalisation projects are underway to use computer-checking in mathematics, such as in Lean, Coq, the HOL family including Isabelle, and Mizar. These all have different implementations of how proofs are written and how things are formalised. If the successes of these formalisation projects are to be used to support the standard view by vindicating the possibility of formalising mathematics, it seems that we must accept that these systems are capable of justifying rigorous proofs. However, these systems are all idiosyncratic to some extent, and the product of various contingent programming choices, so it is unlikely that they are really explaining the rigour of mathematical proofs.

---

[22] For example, Rav (1999) and Azzouni (2004) disagree on this matter. Weir (2016) argues that allowing proofs to be infinitary is necessary for the standard view.

The proponents of the standard view would point out that the key feature of these various systems is that they should contain enough standard, everyday mathematics. The many systems all prove largely the same things, using mostly the same tools. As Azzouni makes explicit for his derivation-indicator view, the details of the exact system are not important so long as it captures the right inferences. It could also be that any system is fine so long as it satisfies some list of criteria, though I know of no such list. Nonetheless, we have seen that the details are important if the standard view is to explain mathematical rigour.

3.7.2 Incompleteness and Inconsistency

One limitation on formal systems comes from Gödel's two incompleteness theorems. The first shows that any consistent formal system that is sufficient to prove a certain amount of mathematics will fail to be complete, meaning that there will be statements that it cannot prove or disprove. The second then proves that, if such a formal system is consistent, then the statement that the system is consistent will not be provable within the system. Gödel's proofs involve using a coding to construct a Gödel sentence G_F (relative to a formal system F), which is provably equivalent to the formula expressing that G_F is unprovable in the system F. The sentence G_F will not be provable in F, on pain of contradiction, but will therefore be true of the system F.

Priest (1987, ch. 2), who wants to argue for dialetheism – the view that there are true contradictions – and, in support of this, that mathematics is inherently inconsistent, uses the standard view as a main premise of his argument. The idea is that if one takes the standard view seriously, then rigorous informal proof procedures can be formalised, and hence can be used to generate an inconsistency using Gödel's theorems:

> For let T be (the formalisation of) our naïve proof procedures. Then, since T satisfies the conditions of Gödel's theorem, if T is consistent there is a sentence φ which is not provable in T, but which we can establish as true by a naïve proof, and hence is provable in T. The only way out of the problem, other than to accept the contradiction, and thus dialetheism anyway, is to accept the inconsistency of naïve proof. So we are forced to admit that our naïve proof procedures are inconsistent. But our naïve proof procedures just are those methods of deductive argument by which things are established as true. It follows that some contradictions are true; that is, dialetheism is correct. (Priest 1987, p. 44)

In my own work (Tanswell 2016a), I have argued that the place where this argument breaks is in adopting the standard view in the first place.

A proponent of the standard view is therefore challenged to offer a different solution, or to accept Priest's conclusion that mathematics is inconsistent.

3.7.3 Unformalisable proofs and Faithfulness

A major strategy for attacking the standard view has been to present proofs that would appear to be unformalisable. If there exists a rigorous proof that is unformalisable, this would be a counterexample to the standard view. Likely candidates would be diagrammatic proofs or proofs that rely essentially on diagrams.[23] However, while these may be hard to capture in language-based formal systems, there are formal systems for certain kinds of diagrams too, such as Mumma's (2010) formal system for Euclid's Elements and Shin's (1994) systems *Venn-I* and *Venn-II*. This suggests that rigorous diagrams could be amenable to treatment by a formal system for diagrams. Nonetheless, De Toffoli (2023) shows that there are rigorous diagrammatic proofs that cannot be faithfully translated into formal counterparts.

Likewise, recall the proof by "Gestalt shift". It may not be possible to capture faithfully reasoning that relies on such a switch of perspective.[24] However, the word "faithfully" is important here, because with the resources of formal logic a great many things are formalisable in some broad sense, but in trying to underwrite a rigorous informal proof we want the formalisation to be faithful to the reasoning pattern of the original.[25] Faithfulness will mean something like preserving the main ideas, structure, and methods of the proof. To the critic of the standard view, it may be obvious that a translation should be faithful in order to secure rigour, but for the proponent this requirement could be seen as unfairly restricting the tools of logic by setting a nebulous extra requirement on translation. After all, who judges the faithfulness of a translation, and by what standards?[26]

---

[23] Azzouni (2020) argues against the standard view along these lines, with a recent reply by Weisgerber (2022).

[24] The specific version we saw was given as an example of an unrigorous but correct proof, so this suggests that this example could be rejected. However, there is no obvious reason why there could not be a rigorous proof by Gestalt shift. Even the one we saw could be made more explicit while still relying on the Gestalt shift as its main strategy, and it is this move that seems to be difficult to formalise faithfully. In Sangwin and Tanswell (2023) we also look at the process of translating back and forth between algebraic and diagrammatic proofs.

[25] The significance of faithfulness of translations in the literature might be traced to Lakatos (1976). For example: "Alpha: Are you sure that your translation of 'polyhedron' into vector theory was a *true* translation?" (Lakatos 1976, p. 121). I will discuss this book in Section 3.

[26] This problem is also considered by De Toffoli (2023) who rightly points out that identity conditions for proofs are hard to pin down and are context-dependent.

3.7.4 Knowledge and Explanatory Redundancy

A main line of attack from mathematical practice on the standard view has been epistemic, arguing that formal proofs are not needed to explain how informal rigorous proofs provide mathematical knowledge. That is: formal proofs are explanatorily redundant in the epistemology of mathematics.[27]

Rav (1999) lists various areas of mathematics that are accepted as rigorous and proceed without axiomatisation or formalisation as an intermediary.[28] Therefore, as a descriptive account of how rigour secures mathematical knowledge in practice, it does not succeed. The three more advanced versions of the standard view would reply that their models are necessary to explain rigour as a normative ideal for proof, and that the actual practices are trying to meet this ideal in various ways. Nonetheless, other literature challenges these solutions. For example, replying to the *routine translations* view, Weber (2023) gives two examples from computability theory where proofs are taken to be rigorous by the mathematical community, but are not verifiable by mathematicians in the way Hamami has set out, nor are the techniques developed in the cumulative way that he describes.

Similarly, Antonutti Marfori (2010) argues that the lack of formalisations in mathematical practice, either in presenting proofs or resolving controversies about proofs, means that an epistemic account based on formalisation would make mathematical knowledge mysterious. Either this leaves mathematical practice "lazy and unsuccessful" (Antonutti Marfori 2010, p. 267) or it allows informal proofs to track mathematical truth without the practitioners knowing how, which makes for an unconvincing account of mathematical knowledge.

Pelc (2009) also argues that formal proofs might be too long to play a role in mathematical knowledge. In practice, formalisations are longer than their informal counterparts. Pelc argues that for complicated proofs, such as Wiles's proof of Fermat's Last Theorem, it is not known whether the formalisation is so long that it would ever be verifiable, even if all the resources in the universe were dedicated to the task.[29] Therefore, formal

---

[27] Besides those listed in the text, Buldt et al. (2008) use this argument as a launch pad for demanding a new epistemology of mathematics that does not rely on the standard view. Goethe and Friend (2010) also give a version of this argument.

[28] The list of "unaxiomatised" theories Rav (1999, p. 16–18) gives now looks rather quaint because in the intervening years a lot more formal mathematics has been done, and many of the listed areas have been formalised and verified in systems like Lean and Mizar. This doesn't undermine Rav's point, though, which is that the mathematical practices were perfectly fine and rigorous without those formalisations.

[29] Freek Wiedijk has a list tracking the formalisation efforts of 100 "top" theorems in various formal systems, in an exercise to follow developments in formal mathematics (www.cs.ru.nl/~freek/100/). Funnily enough, the only theorem that has not yet been formalised in any of the main systems is Fermat's Last Theorem. The fact that the other 99 haven't seen the humongous

proofs cannot be playing an active role in the actual mathematical knowledge mathematicians have.

Müller-Hill (2009) substantiates this criticism with an empirical study of mathematicians' intuitions about mathematical knowledge and formalisability. In her study, she asked 76 respondents who had some experience in teaching or researching mathematics about various vignettes and whether the characters have mathematical knowledge or not, testing what kind of proof access is considered necessary or sufficient for mathematical knowledge.[30] The most interesting result concerns a vignette in which a proposed proof of a famous conjecture is published after a favourable referee report, at which point 84.9 per cent of respondents considered the author "John" to know that the theorem was true. However, the next vignette has John attend a talk five years later which reveals the possibility of constructing counterexamples to the conjecture he had proved. Now, 61.3 per cent of participants agreed that he knows the conjecture to be false. Amazingly, after the existence of a counterexample had been introduced as part of the example, participants were asked whether John knew the conjecture was true on the morning before the talk, and 71 per cent said that he did. This seems to ascribe knowledge to John of something false, contrary to the received wisdom from epistemology that knowledge entails truth. Examining the open-text replies that Müller-Hill (2009, p. 289) reports, we might speculate that participants were not drawing a sharp distinction between knowledge and some internalist kind of justified belief. That is, John was both justified in believing the theorem in the morning, and justified in believing it to be false after the talk. Müller-Hill's own conclusion from these responses is that mathematicians are not invoking a formalisability condition for mathematical knowledge because the proof is judged to be sufficient for John to have mathematical knowledge, but since it must contain an error it also cannot be formalisable.

3.7.5 Overgeneration

Another argument, which I have set out myself as the "overgeneration" objection (Tanswell 2015), is that the success of formal mathematics shows that formalisation can also be *too easy* to support the standard view. An informal proof

---

explosion in size after formalisation does not contradict Pelc's point that the mere possibility of them being too long is enough to show they are not playing an active role in mathematical epistemology.

[30] Perhaps concerningly for us, Müller-Hill (2011, p. 279) also reports that only 10 of 76 respondents thought that philosophers would be best placed to know what mathematical knowledge is, compared to 75 who thought mathematicians were. But participants were allowed to select multiple options!

overgenerates formal counterparts because there are many different ways to formalise even simple pieces of reasoning. The availability of multiple, substantially different formal proofs corresponding to the same informal proof puts pressure on the idea that the correspondence can explain rigour. In the paper, I consider the example of the *mutilated chess board problem*: to cover a chess board that is missing its two opposite corners (see Figure 5) with dominoes that would cover two squares each. The simple proof that this is impossible is based on the fact that any domino will cover two *different* colour squares, so to be coverable there need to be the same number of squares of each colour. But the removed corners are the *same* colour meaning that there are more squares of one colour than another, so they cannot be covered by the dominoes.

The crux of the overgeneration argument is contrasting three substantially different formalisations of this intuitively clear proof. If the rigour of the informal argument *depends* on formal counterparts, then it is puzzling how this dependence could be on many different formal proofs. If we view formalisation as a complex and creative process carried out by mathematicians – among others – as opposed to mechanically extracting what is already implicit in the informal proof, then the idea that formalisation is tracking some objective way that rigour depends on formal derivations seems highly implausible.

Once again, an implicit assumption here is that the formalisation must be faithfully capturing the "true essence" of the informal proof. I think a lot of the explanatory work for the standard view (on both rigour and correctness) is done on the general belief that formalisation is capturing the true essence of the proof. Real formalisation projects have been hugely successful at actually formalising proofs, but they cannot maintain the "true essence" idea because multiple distinct formalisations will track different ways of formalising a proof, with different ways of reasoning, dependencies, assumptions, and details.

Figure 5 The mutilated chess board. Edited from a public domain image from Wikimedia Commons, uploaded by user Ovinus.

One possible reply to this overgeneration argument is that an informal proof is rigorous so long as there exists even one formal correspondent, so there being multiple such correspondents does not undermine the view (e.g., Avigad 2021, p. 7387). But this misunderstands the criticism. The point is that the correspondence between informal and formal proof is doing a great deal of philosophical work for the various versions of the standard view. The correspondence relation between them is such that the rigour on the informal side depends on and is explained by the formal side. The criticism is that this kind of dependence is not tracked by the process of formalisation, because the multiple different formal proofs cannot all be the *explanation* for the rigour of the informal proof. In sum, there may be many formalisations of an informal proof, but their multiplicity undermines their explanatoriness.

3.7.6 The Mismatch Argument

Another criticism focusing on the process of formalisation is what we can call the *mismatch* argument, which is that there is a mismatch between rigorous informal proofs and formalisable ones. The standard view would see them as equivalent, so if they do not match up correctly then there is a problem. First of all, an informal proof that fails to be rigorous might be formalisable anyway. Such a proof would contain either gaps or errors. Gaps are already fixed in the process of formalisation (recall "filling in the gaps"), so gappy proofs are formalisable. It would be hard to draw a firm and principled line between gaps that can be routinely filled in and those that are substantial enough to declare a proof to be unrigorous. But what is there to stop someone involved in formalising a proof from also fixing errors they come across? Indeed, this is how formalisation is seen to work, even by proponents of the standard view: "To be sure, the formalization process sometimes uncovers minor errors and omissions in the informal presentation that have to be remedied, but these are conventionally viewed as just that – errors and omissions – rather than indications that the informal source is correct but unformalizable" (Avigad 2021, p. 7379).

On the contrary, these suggest to me that the proof is formalisable but not correct. These kinds of cases can occur when a theorem is true, but the proof is flawed. Note that the proponent of the standard view, in trying to explain **Correctness**, does not, strictly speaking, have an independent characterisation of errors to fall back on because this is precisely what is at issue. This means they cannot wholesale rule out fixing errors from the intended formalisation process. That proofs with errors can be formalisable is thus a serious concern.

Conversely, what happens when mathematicians are unable to formalise a proof? Does this reveal that the informal proof was unrigorous or incorrect, or is it that they need to continue to work at the formalisation? Indeed, it may be possible that a different mathematician would be able to formalise the proof after all. The answer, then, comes down to whether one believes the informal proof is correct and rigorous in the first place. However, the explanatory order is then the opposite of the standard view: our intuitions of formalisability are explained by our judgements of informal rigour. This would leave the standard view not as an explanation, but as a post hoc rationalisation.

3.7.7 Larvor's Regress

Larvor (2016) makes a quick argument that the standard view faces a regress problem. He observes that the existence of a formal derivation in some system is itself a mathematical claim. When a mathematician has informally proved a theorem, then according to the standard view, this acts as an argument for the existence of a corresponding formal proof in a suitable formal system. Indeed, by the standard view this must be a compelling and rigorous argument for the existence of such a formal derivation. However, then the rigorous argument for a mathematical claim must itself be explained by the standard view. If the rigour is to be explained by the existence of yet another derivation, the view faces an unwelcome regress. Must each informal proof in fact be supported by an infinite hierarchy of derivations? Alternatively, one must concede that the informal proof is sufficient to establish the mathematical claim that there exists a formal derivation in a suitable system. But of course, this concedes everything: "Compare this with the more straightforward view that [the informal proof] is as it stands, before any translation into a formal language, an adequate proof of [the theorem]" (Larvor 2016, p. 3). Neither the regress, nor the concession, seem to be palatable to the standard view, so responding to this criticism would involve finding some other way to break the dichotomy; but this strikes me as robust and so the criticism is, in my opinion, formidable.

3.8 True Essences and Modelling

Let us draw our discussion of the standard view to an end. We have by now seen a whole menagerie of criticisms of the standard view laid out. A more detailed discussion of the various versions of the standard view could investigate whether some of them are better able to defend against (or could be modified appropriately to address) some of the criticisms, which is certainly the case.

Such a discussion could also level more specific criticisms against the details of those views. Taken together, though, I believe that the criticisms show that the central idea of the standard view is wrong: that informal rigour cannot depend on formalisation and corresponding derivations. The promise of computer-checkable, gapless, fully correct derivations providing absolute mathematical certainty is understandably appealing, but the philosophical details do not stand up to scrutiny.

However, while I am certainly critical of the standard view on its own terms, we should not be too hasty in abandoning it entirely. Many aspects of the standard view are very sensible. For example, clearly mathematics and logic are closely related, and the idea that when a gap is too large, the author of the proof should be able to give more details is intuitively compelling. Furthermore, treating proofs as formal derivations is central to metamathematical theorems such as incompleteness results, independence results, the work on reverse mathematics, and the mathematical possibilities of using different logics. These results do have a direct influence on practice. For example, if a mathematician discovered that a claim they were trying to prove was equivalent to the continuum hypothesis, it would be a fool's errand to try to prove this *informally* from the axioms of ZFC.

I propose that the way to make sense of this conundrum is with rigour pluralism. Implicit in several of the criticisms of the previous section was the search for the "true essence" of an informal proof in its formal counterpart. I think that the approach of searching for the formal essence of an informal proof is doomed to fail because there is no such essence. However, if we take the alternative view that what is going on is a kind of conceptual modelling (see Löwe & Müller 2011), that different formalisations are different models of informal proofs, and that the family of different versions of the standard view are closely related models of rigour and proof, then we have a more coherent story to tell.

The rigour pluralist, therefore, can happily accept metamathematical results that rely on formal mathematics as telling us about the limits of provability more generally, since this is one of the main purposes of these models of rigour. At the same time, the pluralist is not thereby committed to the unique correctness of the standard view. The move to the pluralistic modelling approach abandons the aim of giving a uniquely correct answer to what mathematical rigour is. This means that not only are there multiple versions of the standard view with different strengths and weaknesses, but there is also a selection of other models of informal rigour that provide different insights. In Sections 4, 5, and 6 we will investigate three other families of models of informal rigour and proofs, and evaluate their virtues and shortcomings.

4 Arguments and Dialogues

4.1 Introduction

In the previous section we saw that formal logic provides a good model for rigorous mathematical proofs, but not without limitations. One thing that is abstracted away by the family of standard views is the social dimension of rigour: the *mathematicians* themselves are largely absent or highly idealised. The other models we will consider in this and the remaining sections include more of those social features of proofs in practice. In this section, we examine a selection of models of rigour that rely on seeing proofs as *arguments* or *dialogues*, where these also involve contextual features like who is arguing, why they are arguing, their attitudes towards what they are arguing over, and the dynamics of the exchange between them.

To begin, I shall look at the application of *argumentation theory* to mathematical proofs. The discipline of argumentation theory is about how arguments work: what kinds of arguments do and do not succeed; how arguments are used to persuade or convince; and what kinds of fallacies arise in argumentation. Argumentation theory and informal logic have long and varied histories, but their modern incarnations address shortcomings of formal logic in explaining real arguments. Addressing the similar shortcomings of formal logic in explaining features of real proofs is an obvious use to put it to. In Section 4.2 we will look at how some of the leading theories from argumentation theory can apply to rigorous proofs, drawing primarily on the extensive work on this by Andrew Aberdein.

In Section 4.3 we will turn to one of the best-known works on proofs as dialogues: Imre Lakatos's (1976) *Proofs and Refutations*. Lakatos proposes a *dialectical model of proofs in mathematics*, with many important ideas that affect how one should understand mathematical rigour. From here, in Section 4.4, we will jump to a very recent model of proofs as dialogues by Catarina Dutilh Novaes (2021) in *The Dialogical Roots of Deduction*. Her proposal is to see deduction, and therefore also deductive mathematical proofs, as fundamentally dialogical.

4.2 Proofs as Arguments

Characterising proofs as a kind of argument has several clear motivations. First of all, empirical work by Davies et al. (2020) has shown that many mathematicians do indeed think of proofs as arguments, so at the very least it fits with the descriptive-normative side of rigour, that is, it matches what mathematicians say they are doing. Second, one of the best-known views of proofs, as defended by Hersh (1993, 1997) is that: "In mathematical practice, in the real life of living mathematicians, *proof is convincing argument, as judged by qualified judges*" (Hersh 1993, p. 389).[31]

Argumentation theory is designed to understand the way in which arguments do this convincing, and under what conditions they succeed and fail. Third, argumentation theory attends to the context of argumentation, such as who is arguing and why, so will include these features of the context for mathematical proving too. Fourth, this discipline has a large catalogue of specific types and patterns of argument that have been analysed, and which can be used to identify specific patterns of argument invoked by mathematicians in an existing taxonomy. Finally, it can tell us about mathematical fallacies, and hence tell us about rigour negatively, by identifying failures of rigour.

One of the leading proponents of analysing mathematics using argumentation theory is Andrew Aberdein (2005, 2006, 2007, 2010, 2013, 2021, 2023). A major contribution he makes is to examine what insights might be gained from two classic models of argumentation by Toulmin (1958) and Walton (1998). Let us consider these in turn.

Toulmin's argumentation model (Figure 6) is designed to make explicit the structure of an argument for a claim *C*, by picking how your starting data *D* will warrant that conclusion. That warrant *W*, may also rely on some backing *B*, to justify it. Furthermore, one should identify the qualifiers *Q*, needed when the warrant is weaker than a logically valid inference, and the conditions under which the inference would be rebutted, *R*.

This generalises to many more possible arguments than formal logic does. As a model of mathematical proofs, though, we might wonder what exactly it adds, since informal rigorous proofs should still be logical to the extent that they do not admit qualifications and rebuttals. The benefit of this approach is shown by Alcolea Banegas (1997/2013) and Aberdein (2007), who look at how Toulmin's model will apply to the computer-aided proof of the Four Colour Theorem (Appel & Haken 1977; Appel et al. 1977; see also

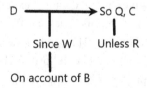

Figure 6 Toulmin's argument model (Toulmin 1958, p. 97).

---

[31] In his second article (Hersh 1997), this becomes: "It is argument which convinces the qualified, skeptical expert" (p. 153). This extra clause will be relevant to the dialogical model we will see shortly.

Secco & Pereira 2017).[32] The idea is that one can make explicit exactly how reliance on the computerised case-enumeration feeds into the overall argument of the proof, such as by identifying the warrant and backing: "(W) The computer has been properly programmed and its hardware has no defects. ... (B) Technology and computer programming are sufficiently reliable" (Alcolea Banegas 1997/2013, p. 55).

Alcolea Banegas then argues that: "since no strictly mathematical warrant is available, the door remains open for a specific counterexample ... Mathematicians find themselves in the uncomfortable situation of having to accept both the fallibility and the indispensability of the computer" (Alcolea Banegas 1977/2013, p. 56). However, Aberdein points out that this reveals a limitation in Toulmin's model, since one could add that the reasoning would be rebutted 'when there has been an error in our reasoning'. Indeed, one could add this to the layout for *any* mathematical proof. Since the case-checking for the Four Colour Theorem has been done multiple times on multiple machines with different software and coding, the likelihood of human error can easily be argued to be higher than that of computer error.[33] The point is that Toulmin's model may still be too detached from important context. In Aberdein's words: "The degree of abstraction necessary to use [Toulmin's model] at all can make different, incompatible, reconstructions possible, leaving the suspicion that any such reconstruction may involve considerable (and unquantified) distortion" (Aberdein 2007, p. 61).

We might also worry that choosing controversial cases of proofs, such as that of the Four Colour Theorem, means that this model is too far removed from *rigorous* proof because it is precisely focused on places where mathematical rigour is lacking. However, it is possible to apply the model to more central examples of informal rigorous proofs. For example, one can analyse an inference within a proof in terms of its warrant and backing, with a domain of validity. In that case, if the backing is sufficiently obvious to the intended audience, then this may be a way to examine rigour without relying on formal logic. Indeed, Aberdein gives more detailed examples of applications of Toulmin's layout to standard proofs, such as the proof of unique prime factorisation (Aberdein 2006, p. 217), the intermediate value theorem (Aberdein 2006, p. 219), and a classic proof about irrational numbers (Aberdein 2005, fig. 4) reproduced here (Figure 7).[34]

---

[32] Alcolea Banegas's original 1997 paper was published in Catalan, then translated into English and republished in 2013.

[33] Indeed, the entire proof of the Four Colour Theorem has been formalised and computer-checked by Gonthier (2008).

[34] The exact claim is that there exist two irrationals α and β such that α^β is rational.

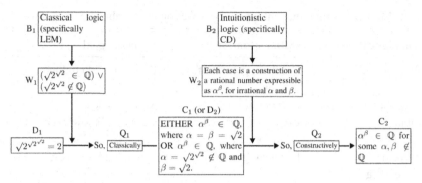

Figure 7 Toulmin's layout for a proof about irrational numbers by Aberdein (2005, fig. 4). This uses the same abbreviations as those cited in this section: Claim (C), Backing (B), Warrant (W), Qualifier (Q), and Data (D).

Note: my thanks to Andrew Aberdein for help with reconstructing this diagram.

In Figure 7, we can see how Toulmin's layout can be modified to fit the chains of reasoning found in proofs, with the conclusion of one argument becoming the data for the second.[35] Also, Aberdein here demonstrates how the layout can be used to show the structure of a proof relying on different logical resources (namely, constructively and classically valid inferences). This makes it possible to analyse the rigour of the argument by bringing out explicitly the dependencies and connections between different parts of the proof.

The second option that Aberdein considers is the model of argument suggested by Walton (1998). Walton's central idea is to see arguments as essentially taking place between arguers, who each start with initial attitudes towards what is being argued about (such as believing it true, false, or unknown) as well as goals for being involved in the argument. This leads to a taxonomy of six argument types, as summarised in Table 1. For example, if one person believes that the proposition they are arguing about is true and the other doesn't know either way, then they might end up in an *information-seeking* dialogue, with the goal of spreading knowledge from one to the other. However, if they disagree, with one believing it is true and one believing it is false, then the type of dialogue will depend on their goals. If they are looking to resolve the conflict, then they may end up in a *persuasion* dialogue, attempting to convince one another. Otherwise, they may enter a *negotiation* to find an adequate compromise for both parties, or they may exchange their views in an *eristic* dialogue (that is, a quarrel) with no hope of a stable resolution. In practice, the kind of

---

[35] This modification was briefly considered by Toulmin himself (Toulmin et al. 1979, sect. 7). Other modifications are considered by Aberdein (2006) and Knipping and Reid (2019).

Table 1 Six main argument types, from Walton and Krabbe (1995, p. 80).

Dialogue type	Initial situation	Dialogue goal
Persuasion	Conflicting point of view	Resolution of conflict
Negotiation	Conflict of interest	Making a deal
Inquiry	General ignorance	Growth of knowledge
Deliberation	Need for action	Reach a decision
Information-seeking	Personal ignorance	Spreading knowledge
Eristic (quarrel)	Antagonism	Accommodation relationship

argument one is engaged in might change over time, moving from one type to another in response to the changing context.

The insight that this taxonomy provides is that an argument can only be properly evaluated in the context of what kind of argument it is, that is, different kinds of arguments have different norms and standards for arguing.

To apply this model to mathematical proofs, Aberdein (2007, p. 64, 2021) points out that the usual perspective would be to see proofs as being special cases of *inquiry*, where the arguers move from mutual ignorance to knowledge via jointly accepted methods of reasoning. However, in practice there are many other potential audiences for a proof. Aberdein lists journal referees, mathematicians in the same field, mathematicians from other fields, students, prospective researchers, and "posterity" as other possible audiences that the prover may be engaged with, with other possible goals. Dealing with journal referees, the situation is more like one of persuasion, or even adversarial. Presenting a proof for students means entering a *pedagogical* dialogue, a subtype of the *information-seeking* dialogue. Aberdein (2007, p. 67) fills out a whole table of mathematical versions of the various dialogue types, reflecting on different ways to interpret proofs and their purposes. Some of these are at odds with rigorous conceptions of proofs, such as Zeilberger's (1993) suggestion to accept "semi-rigorous" results up to a certain degree of certainty, with a price tag for how much it would cost (financially or computationally) to be sure, which Aberdein interprets as viewing proofs as *negotiation* (weighing up how sure we need to be to accept a mathematical statement) or *deliberation* (on how to allocate finite resources for solving problems).

The question that remains is: what does Walton's model mean for rigorous mathematical proofs? Different argumentative contexts are evaluated differently, so if multiple different kinds of dialogues can be associated with proofs, then the standards of rigour may also vary. Perhaps some of the dialogues are simply not good models for mathematical rigour, such as Zeilberger's explicit move away from rigour. There seems to be scope to fill out in further detail how different dialogue types might make different kinds of gaps in proofs acceptable or not, as Aberdein (2013) does, thus giving a more detailed model of rigorous proofs as using different kinds of argumentative moves. In particular, recognising that proofs aiming at pedagogy have different requirements on rigour from those of peer review, or writing for one's mathematical colleagues, is an important feature of these argumentation models of proofs.

4.3 Proofs and Refutations

One of the most influential works on the development of the philosophy of mathematical practice is Imre Lakatos's (1976) *Proofs and Refutations*. Lakatos presents a classroom dialogue about various proofs of "Euler's conjecture" for polyhedra, which links the vertices (V), edges (E), and faces (F) by the formula $V - E + F = 2$. The dialogue is also a "rational reconstruction" of the historical development of the proof attempts, counterexamples, arguments, and concepts relating to this conjecture, where the various students are used as representatives of various historical positions and reactions. Sometimes this is in a very direct sense, with footnotes to the text indicating that the words of the students are quotes from various mathematicians, such as Euler, Poincaré, Cauchy, Abel, Kepler, and many more.

The dialogue begins with a proposed proof of the Euler conjecture that involves removing a face from the polyhedron and using the resulting hole to stretch and flatten it out. Since one face is gone, the remaining flattened network should satisfy $V - E + F = 1$. Next one "triangulates" the network to turn all the faces into triangles by connecting vertices with additional edges. Each extra edge also creates an extra face, so leaves the totals in the Euler formula unaffected. The next step is to remove other faces one at a time, where any option once again leaves the formula unaffected, until just one triangle remains, which satisfies the Euler formula. By tracking the numbers of faces, edges, and vertices throughout this procedure, the idea is that one can conclude that the Euler formula must hold for the network that we started with.

This procedure and the proof seemingly work well enough for simple, convex polyhedra such as the five Platonic solids (tetrahedron, cube, octahedron, dodecahedron, and icosahedron), cuboids, pyramids, or icosidodecahedra. However, things are not so straightforward. The students quickly start to find potential counterexamples to both the main conjecture ("global counterexamples") and to individual proof steps ("local counterexamples"). For instance, a cylinder or a picture frame (see Figure 8) both act as global counterexamples to the conjecture. Furthermore, a cylinder is a local counterexample to the triangulations step of the proof, while the picture frame is a local counterexample to the first step of removing a face and flattening the polyhedron to a network, which can't be done.

The interesting question that follows is: what to do with these counterexamples? One could simply give up on the proof altogether, but that seems to discard some promising mathematics involved in the procedure that does work for plenty of examples. One can instead question whether these counterexamples really count as polyhedra at all, maybe excluding them as "monsters" that don't need to be dealt with once we have a better definition. After all, the cylinder has a curved face and circular edges; maybe these should exclude it from being a polyhedron. One could try to discover the appropriate domain for which the proof does work: could it be that the proof is just about convex polyhedra?

A particularly important counterexample is the star-polyhedron (see Figure 8). This is initially proposed as a counterexample made up of 12 interlocking "star-pentagons" as faces, with 12 vertices (only the tips) and 30 edges, whereby $V - E + F = -6$. However, an alternative way of seeing it would be as being made up of 60 triangular faces, and on this interpretation it does satisfy the Euler formula after all. The proof attempt thus forces the students to confront their definitions of polyhedron, face, vertex, and edge. The developments of these definitions are therefore related to one another, but also depend on the context of the Euler conjecture and the attempted proof. For instance, one might be inclined to prefer the triangle-faces interpretation *because* it allows for

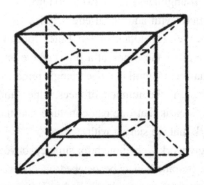

Figure 8 Lakatos's picture frame (Lakatos 1976, p. 19) and Kepler's star-polyhedron (Lakatos 1976, p. 17). © Cambridge University Press.

the proof procedure to be coherently carried out, whereas the star-pentagon interpretation does not.

The crucial insight by Lakatos is that working with proposed proofs and potential counterexamples drives the development of mathematical concepts by forcing mathematicians to address questions about what those concepts are, how they are used, and what they are used for. Lakatos's project involves developing a *dialectical* philosophy of mathematics.[36] According to Larvor (2001), a dialectical philosophy of mathematics has a number of characteristic features. First of all, it focuses on processes rather than products, which means that that the relevant questions about proof are not about truth or validity, but instead about how the proof came about, or what roles it plays in further mathematical activity. Second, the dialectical model will focus on the development of *concepts*, as opposed to the inferential moves between *propositions* which are the standard subject of formal logic. So, on the dialectical model, concepts are changed and refined via mathematical activity.[37] Third, these developments are rational within mathematics itself, which Larvor (2001, p. 215) calls the "inside-phenomenological stance". Simply put: mathematical developments (such as of concepts, ideas, or theories) happen for good mathematical reasons, as judged from within mathematics.

In combination, these features of a dialectical model of proofs mean that the dialectical notion of *rigour* will come apart from the formal notion of rigour that we saw in Section 3. The dialectical model of rigour will be about the process of mathematics, and the rational development of concepts that goes along with it. One way to put this is to contrast this dynamical concept of rigour with a more standard, static concept of rigour, as Kneebone does: "In other words for the purposes of philosophy we have to conceive of rigour in dynamical not in statical terms – as the rigour of a *process* which yields knowledge, not of a system of propositions which summarize a particular *state* of knowledge" (Kneebone 1957, p. 223).

However, having this pair of concepts of rigour leads to a problem. One of the main purposes of rigorous proofs is to establish theorems, but if the concepts being used in a proof can change, then it is also possible for the proof to rely on

---

[36] The work of Lakatos is commonly seen as an unholy marriage of the work of Hegel (1807) and Popper (1959, 1963), with the dialectical parts coming from the former. An earlier, and overlooked, proposal to develop a dialectical philosophy of mathematics in the spirit of Hegel was made by Kneebone (1957) but this lacks the crucial account of just how mathematics is dialectical that Lakatos provides.

[37] The recent literature on *conceptual engineering* is precisely about how concepts can be revised or replaced. I have investigated conceptual engineering in the case of mathematics, and in relation to Lakatos, in earlier work (Tanswell 2018).

a false equivocation, using properties of one version of the concept at one point in the proof, and properties of another variation on the concept at some other point. If this were the case, then the proof is fallacious and fails at its goal of establishing theorems and providing mathematical knowledge.

Recent literature has provided various possible solutions to this puzzle.[38] One option is to try to identify some subset of concepts that will not be open to change, so that proofs using only those concepts can be deductively rigorous. Vecht (2023) argues that in mathematics algebraic concepts are fully fixed, where algebraic definitions are ones that do not assert the existence of any objects, but instead say that any structure satisfying the definition counts. For example, *group* and *natural number* have algebraic definitions, so proofs about these can be rigorous in the deductive sense. Another option is to separate out the contexts where concepts are fixed and rigid from those where they are flexible. Schlimm (2012) takes this pluralistic approach, suggesting that some parts of mathematics and its history are best understood using a Lakatosian dialectical model, while others are better modelled using fixed, unchanging concepts. Presumably, it is proofs in the latter contexts that are deductively rigorous, but proofs outside of that context may still be informative and mathematical in other ways. Another option is to see the conceptual flexibility as a feature of informal, unrigorous mathematics that is removed by rigorisation or formalisation. This approach is considered by both Shapiro and Roberts (2021) and Zayton (2022) and also fits with the second chapter of *Proofs and Refutations* itself. After one has formalised away the conceptual flexibility, though, new questions arise about the adequacy and faithfulness of the formalisation.

Lakatos's own perspective seems to be that there is no hope of sanitised mathematics, free from the dialectical change of concepts:

> Delta: *Rationality, after all, depends on inelastic, exact, concepts!*

> Kappa: *But there are no such concepts! Why not accept that our ability to specify what we mean is nil, therefore our ability to prove is nil?* If you want mathematics to be meaningful, you must resign of certainty. You cannot have both. *Gibberish is safe from refutations, meaningful propositions are refutable by concept-stretching.* (Lakatos 1976, p. 102)[39]

I have likewise argued that there are no safe havens for mathematical concepts where mathematicians have full control over their meanings

---

[38] This literature combines the Lakatosian point with the question of whether mathematical concepts are *open-textured*, a term from Friedrich Waismann (1968), roughly meaning that there will always be possible cases for which it is unsettled whether they fall under the concept or not.

[39] The italics here, from the original, are used to indicate that the dialogue is at this point pretty heated.

(Tanswell 2018). Nonetheless, I believe the equivocation threat to proofs posed by changing concepts is rather overblown. For changing concepts to cause a fallacy of equivocation within a proof requires that the concepts change from one usage to the next within that very proof and in a way relevant to the reasoning in the proof. The simple solution is that the dialectical change of concepts does not happen so quickly, nor at this level of detail. Concepts don't change within proofs, precisely because this would lead to a failure of deductive rigour, but proofs as a whole do drive the dialectical development of concepts. Actually, the level of individual proofs is likely still too fine-grained for the dialectical model; instead, mathematical communities together are negotiating, developing, refining, and replacing the concepts that are being used in their practices. But this also means that if new changes in a concept invalidate some previously accepted proof, then it is down to the mathematical community to be aware of that and either disambiguate the concepts, update the proof, or rein in the concepts. Given a sufficiently large community, with reasonable levels of expertise and shared standards, this task of self-checking on changing concepts doesn't need to be particularly demanding, and certainly doesn't pose a mortal danger to mathematical rigour, be it deductive or dialectical.

4.4 The Dialogical Model of Proofs

The final model we will examine in this section is Catarina Dutilh Novaes's (2021) *dialogical model of proof.* Dutilh Novaes's central claim is that deduction is an essentially dialogical notion. Therefore, deductive mathematical proofs are also essentially dialogical. This model has broad application, as both a historical claim about the genealogy of the concept of deduction (from Ancient Greece through the Middle Ages and Modern period to our current understanding), a model of both normative and descriptive aspects of human reasoning and cognition, and to explain collective reasoning in groups. Finally, it provides a powerful model of mathematical proofs, both as idealised, abstract pieces of reasoning and as real-world products in practice.

The dialogical model of deduction is based on the idea that a piece of deductive reasoning can best be understood as a dialogue between two characters: *Prover* and *Sceptic*. The goal of Prover is to show some claim that is to be proved follows from other claims, first by asking Sceptic to grant various premises, then by putting forward further statements that purportedly follow deductively from previously accepted ones. The goal of Sceptic is to block the conclusion from being established, but not at all costs. Sceptic's moves provide counterexamples to Prover's moves when they do not properly follow, or ask for extra clarification and "why?" questions of steps that are not sufficiently clear or persuasive.

One of Dutilh Novaes's insights is that these dialogues are *semi*-cooperative, rather than purely adversarial. At one level, the goals of Prover and Sceptic are incompatible because either the proof is successful or it fails. At another level, though, their shared goal is to ensure that all and only good proofs are accepted. Prover must do their best at getting good proofs accepted, while making them perspicuous and explanatory, and Sceptic must do their best to block bad proofs. Neither of them is looking to win at all costs, meaning Sceptic does not stubbornly refuse to accept premises or endlessly ask for further clarification just for the sake of winning, nor does Prover want to win deceptively by presenting persuasive but fallacious inferences. This means that Prover also wants the steps they propose to be convincing and explanatory, and Sceptic helps to make sure a proof is perspicuous and clear.

This model can be used at a very basic level to explain logical deduction. For example, Sceptic should only grant the conjunction $(A \wedge B)$ when they have previously granted both A and B, and grant $(A \rightarrow B)$ if it has been shown that assuming A gets to B through valid inferences. The model can also be used for higher-level mathematical proofs, by stipulating that Sceptic will be convinced by standard mathematical inferences (namely, those that are familiar and acceptable to both Prover and Sceptic) without demanding full logical detail.

Dutilh Novaes argues that the Prover–Sceptic dialogical model of deduction explains three core features of deductive arguments. First of all, the property of *necessary truth preservation* is explained in game-theoretic terms of strategy: if Prover only makes necessarily truth-preserving moves, then there can be no counterexamples, so Sceptic cannot block the proof in this way. Second, the property that each step should be *clear and convincing*, is explained by the cooperative nature of the dialogues, because Prover wants to convince Sceptic, not just win the game. Finally, the property of *belief bracketing*, that deduction should be about the connection between premises and conclusion regardless of whether one believes them, flows naturally from the dialogical game of proposing and granting premises, where the whole point is to reason about the granted premises of one's interlocutor without having to believe them oneself.

One immediate objection is that modern proofs are mostly not dialogues, since they do not have two participants at all. Maybe there are some exceptions, like in a seminar or classroom, but most proofs are written as if by a single author, even when the proofs are collaborative. Dutilh Novaes's reply to this is that modern proofs have *internalised* the role of the Sceptic:

Skeptic becomes an *implicit interlocutor*, as it were, given that his main roles in Prover–Skeptic dialogues become constitutive of the deductive method as such. We no longer hear the voice of Skeptic because, if all goes well and the proof is correctly formulated according to the precepts of the deductive method, there is no need for Skeptic to interject. (Dutilh Novaes 2021, p. 70)

The idea is that the way that proofs are written does not need to be explicitly dialogical, because the Prover–Sceptic dialogue is already implicit in how proofs are structured and presented.

Next, let us consider what the dialogical model can tell us about *rigorous* proofs. A rigorous proof comes about when Prover wins, but Sceptic has carried out their role extremely thoroughly. No step has counterexamples that Sceptic missed, so there are no errors in the proof. There are also no gaps in the proof because Sceptic would've asked for further clarification. Unlike in the standard view, this doesn't mean a rigorous proof must be formal. The standards for what counts as a gap – and therefore also the "granularity" of the proof – can vary by context. This would fit well with empirical findings such as those of Davies et al. (2021), who interviewed mathematicians about how they would evaluate various proofs across different contexts. They found that the context of the author makes a substantial difference: mathematicians are far more accepting of gaps in proofs if these are produced by other mathematicians in lectures or textbooks. Indeed, they spoke of these positively as inviting students to ask questions and think for themselves about why the "missing" steps work. Furthermore, even in evaluating students' work, mathematicians grade differently in the context of homework, class quizzes, or final exams. They also explicitly said that the level of rigour they demand from their students is connected to the level of the class they are teaching. For instance, one participant said:

There are times when you give them examples in class that have a certain level of rigor, but as time goes on and as the students become more mature in their own abilities to reason and argue ... you can make statements and assumptions that they have an obligation to sit down and figure out what the details are or know what the implied statements are within that. (Davies et al. 2021, p. 9)

A formal proof might be the limit case of a pedantic Sceptic demanding full detail, but on the dialogical model the Sceptic is also cooperative with the Prover, so this limit case is not always the ideal. Instead, it is often in the cooperative interests of the Prover and Sceptic to rigorously establish that the theorem holds with as few steps as possible, to not waste their time filling out inferences that are obvious to them both. Likewise, as the quote suggests, the optimum level of detail for rigour might vary substantially by context.

In the closing chapter of her book, Dutilh Novaes (2021, ch. 11) looks at three examples of the dialogical model as applied to actual mathematical practice. Without going into the details of her examples, the main point is that the social aspects of proof-checking in practice can be modelled dialogically. In particular, seemingly surprising claims like Gödel's incompleteness theorems, Edward Nelson's failed proof of the inconsistency of Peano Arithmetic, and Shinichi Mochizuki's purported proof of the *abc* conjecture stimulate the mathematical community into scrutinising the claims.[40] The author of the proof acts as Prover while the members of the community examining the proof act as Sceptic. Depending on how the claim is presented, they can sometimes quickly reach a consensus on the correctness of a proof, such as happened in the first two examples. However, at other times, when a proposed proof is less clear, the dialogue between Prover and Sceptic can get trickier, as in the third example, which at the time of writing is still unsettled.[41]

4.5 Conclusion

In this section, we have seen a family of models of rigorous proofs based on argumentation and dialogue, including Toulmin and Walton's argumentation models applied to mathematics, Lakatos's dialectical model of mathematics, and Dutilh Novaes's dialogical model of proof.

One strength of this family of models is that they are more descriptively adequate than the standard view for mathematical practice. By emphasising the role of the mathematicians as interlocutors in a dialogue or argument, the model begins to account for important features of rigour in practice. For example, these models have a clear story about why rigour varies by context; why the rigour of a proof in a classroom, seminar, textbook, journal article, or scribbled on a napkin is evaluated differently. Similarly, the argumentation model can explain why there can be disagreement about rigour or validity or proofs, since different arguers might not agree on the operative proof standards in the current context.

A major benefit of these models is also that they can account for mathematical rigour while also giving a convincing overarching story about the history and development of mathematical concepts. The dialectical model of mathematics sees concepts as developed through mathematical activities, including

---

[40] Crucially, these claims are by well-known and respected mathematicians. For outsiders, it can be much harder to get the community to engage with your work at all (see Rittberg 2023).

[41] For a detailed account of the unfolding story of Mochizuki's purported proof so far, see Aberdein (2023). I also wrote about this case from a virtue-theoretic perspective (Tanswell 2016b, ch. 5.8). Even calling this "unsettled" is not neutral, as different groups have different attitudes to the proof's status.

proving, while the dialogical model offers the view that deduction itself emerged from dialogical roots. While the standard view has to jump through hoops to explain how proofs could be said to have been rigorous prior to the invention of modern logic, the models we have seen here explain this directly.

One thing that is not settled by the argumentation or dialogical models is the nature of diagrammatic proofs. Argumentation and dialogue are – at least primarily – linguistic, and so the models do not obviously apply to proofs that are entirely pictorial, or hybrids of picture and prose. It is possible that one could modify a mathematical argumentation model to take non-propositional premises, or the Prover–Sceptic model to include diagrammatic moves, but this is yet to be done.

Overall, the family of models we have seen here is extremely good at including some aspects of the social context of mathematics without thereby giving up on rigour as an ideal for proofs.

5 The Recipe Model of Proofs

5.1 Introduction

The next model we turn to is the *recipe model of proofs*, and it's one I have developed in my own work (Tanswell 2016b, ch. 4, in press) and with collaborators Keith Weber (Weber & Tanswell 2022) and Matthew Inglis (Tanswell & Inglis 2023), building on work by Larvor (2012). The idea is to understand proofs via an analogy to cooking recipes: that proofs provide a set of instructions for carrying out a particular kind of mathematical activity. The recipe model invites a switch of perspective, whereby the proofs as written artefacts become secondary to the activity and the sequence of actions that they instruct the reader to carry out. Just like a recipe is a way of communicating and recording practical knowledge of how to prepare something to eat, a proof is a way of recording and communicating practical knowledge of how to carry out some piece of mathematical reasoning. A proof also has ingredients, in the form of the prerequisite assumptions and definitions, which list which concepts, facts, and mathematical objects can be called upon in the course of the proof. This could be given a stronger constructivist reading, where the recipe has to be for constructing some mathematical object, but the model does not assume this in general, nor is it limited to constructive proofs.

There are three primary motivations for the recipe model. First, the model makes sense of a number of features of how proofs are written and presented, such as how the language of written proofs includes explicit instructions, and how diagrams can succeed as proofs. Second, the emphasis on mathematical activity allows for a different and broader analysis of the place of rigorous proofs in mathematical practice. Third, the recipe model provides a clear answer to the epistemic question of how we gain knowledge from mathematical proofs. In this section, we will survey all of these facets of the recipe model of proofs.

5.2 Imperatives and Instructions

Let us begin with the language of mathematical proofs. There is a huge range of proof styles and presentations across mathematical cultures and the history of mathematics, and a full survey would fill multiple volumes. I will here consider the linguistic patterns used in contemporary, English mathematics.[42] The proposal is that the way in which proofs are typically written by mathematicians tells us what proofs and rigour are in contemporary mathematical practice. In particular, many theorists characterise a proof as being a logically structured sequence of *assertions*, beginning with accepted premises and proceeding by established inference rules to a conclusion. However, in practice this is often not how proofs are written, as proofs also contain imperative sentences to provide instructions for reasoning. A sentence is in the imperative mood when it forms a command or instructions, such as "Watch out!", "Preheat the oven to 200 degrees", or "Compose the two bijections".

Matthew Inglis and I have recently carried out a corpus linguistics study of mathematical proof texts (Tanswell & Inglis 2023) to examine the frequency with which proofs contain imperatives. By looking at the word distributions in 6,988 preprint research papers from the ArXiv (an online repository that many mathematicians use to circulate their work prior to publication), we found that proofs in research mathematics do frequently contain imperatives. The most common imperatives used the verbs `let', `consider', `assume', `denote', `note', `define', `suppose', `recall', `write', `take', `choose', `fix', and `observe' in that order of prevalence. Furthermore, there was a lot of diversity in the verbs that could be used across different areas of mathematics, suggesting that the writing of mathematical proofs is flexible in allowing instructions to be used. We interpreted these results as showing that imperative sentences were both common and diverse in mathematical proofs. Similarly, Weber (2023) carried out an analysis of all of the proofs in an introductory set theory textbook by Kunen

---

[42] For a discussion of some of the ethical problems of the dominance of English in mathematics, see Tanswell and Rittberg (2020). In particular, we discuss the way that learning the language of academic English used in mathematics presents an extra challenge in learning mathematics for students who don't have English as their first language or who speak dialects. These traits and language challenges map on to existing patterns of power and dominance, and because mathematics is also used to rank attainment and thereby affects life opportunities, the dominance of the English language also perpetuates existing power structures. Another concern about English as lingua franca in science is raised by Vučković and Sikimić (2023), who argue that it leads to linguistic injustice and the loss of diverse ideas.

(1980), finding that 95 per cent of the substantial proofs contained one or more instructions. He also found a similar pattern of a core of 13 instructions being most common, making up 88 per cent of instructions, though not quite the same ones.[43] Furthermore, he found the same pattern of diverse instructions, with 54 different instructions appearing in the textbook.

The recipe model proposes to take this instructional language in proofs seriously, rather than paraphrase or idealise it away (as would be the strategy for the standard view discussed in Section 3). By doing so, this approach can start to analyse how instructions function in proofs. Specifically, different instructions seem to serve different kinds of purposes in a proof, and a detailed understanding of proofs would involve identifying these purposes and analysing how they are achieved while maintaining rigour.

One way to divide the instructions used in proofs was proposed by Brian Rotman (1988) who distinguished between "inclusive" and "exclusive" imperatives. His idea is that the function of "inclusive imperatives" is to establish a shared domain of meanings, referents, conventions, and nomenclature, usually with the instructions "Let . . .", "Suppose . . .", "Fix . . .", "Assume . . .", and the like. The "exclusive imperatives" then operate within that domain to ask the reader to carry out particular actions, like "Differentiate the function f".

Weber (2023) builds on Rotman's distinction with three additional categories. He notes that Rotman's exclusive instructions operate on mathematical objects, instructing the reader to manipulate or use them in some way. Weber thus introduces the category of "inference instructions", which act instead on assertions, such as instructing the reader to apply some previously established fact, or show that something is true by constructing a sub-proof. For example, "Apply Theorem 2.15 . . ." would be an inference instruction. The other two categories Weber proposes are "observational instructions", which instruct the reader to notice a particular fact (e.g., "Observe that . . .", "Note that . . .", "Recall that . . ."), and "reference instructions", used to direct readers to another part of the text using "See [reference]".

These different categories of instructions in proof are clearly relevant to how proofs function, how they are understood, and how they can be rigorous. For example, the existence of the category of observational instructions implies that informal proofs may make use of salience, that is, bringing certain facts to the readers' attention in order to use them as part of the reasoning. These features of

---

[43] 'Denote', 'recall', 'write', and 'take' were replaced by 'see', 'apply', 'pick', and 'use'. This can largely be explained by the textbook being by one particular author, so reflecting his own stylistic preferences. For example, 'recall' and 'see' will often be interchangeable, as will 'take' and 'use'. Academic papers and textbooks have somewhat different purposes and target audiences, which could also explain slight differences in the writing.

attention and salience may then be directly relevant to how the reader understands the proof. Furthermore, the distinction between instructions that act on mathematical objects and those that act on mathematical propositions suggests different kinds of activities are taking place in carrying out the reasoning. Consequently, we would also expect that the different instructions may be rigorous (or not, as the case may be) in different ways. We will return to the question of rigour in Section 5.6.

5.3 Diagrams and Instructions

Instructions are not limited to written language. Human communication comes in many forms, and instructions can be given and understood in many ways. One thing the recipe model can do well is account for otherwise puzzling features of diagrams in proofs, with the idea that some features of diagrams are acting as instructions.[44]

A common challenge in dealing with diagrams in proofs is that more traditional views of proofs as sequences of assertions would require that the diagrammatic elements should be convertible into a sequence of propositions, but how this conversion should work is unclear. With the recipe model of proofs, one can dismiss this requirement as overly narrow. Instead, proofs are about providing directions to engage in a piece of mathematical reasoning, and diagrams can provide those instructions directly. In particular, according to the recipe model, we can understand various explicit and presentational features of diagrams as giving instructions.[45]

For example, consider the diagrammatic proof of Pythagoras's Theorem (Figure 9). Here, the arrows are used explicitly to instruct us to scale up the initial triangle by the three factors, and to rotate and combine them into two larger triangles.[46] My analysis of this proof would be that it instructs us how to transform the initial triangle to build up the two new triangles, then to see that they are mirror images of one another, so will have the same length hypotenuse. No formal or linguistic counterpart is needed.

For a more implicit set of instructions, consider this proof that the sum of odd positive integers add up to a square (Figure 10).

---

[44] A recent study by Blåsjö (2022) argues that ancient Greek geometry was primarily about constructing things. His *operationalism* for the ancient Greeks is very similar in spirit to the recipe model.

[45] In other work (Tanswell 2017, in press), I compare mathematical diagrams to familiar cases of using diagrams to give instructions such as for LEGO® sets and IKEA furniture. On my understanding, these diagrams all work fundamentally in the same ways.

[46] The volumes by Nelsen (1993, 2000, 2015) fall into the category of "recreational" mathematics, so being slightly cryptic is part of the fun.

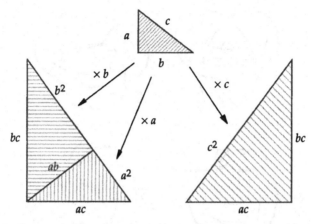

Figure 9 Pythagoras's Theorem adapted by Nelsen from an idea by Frank Burk (see Nelsen 2000, p. 7). Proof Without Words II © 2000 held by the American Mathematical Society.

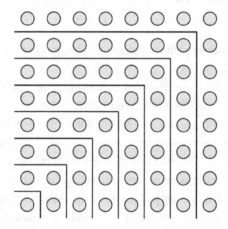

Figure 10 Proof of the sum of odd positive integers credited to Nicomachus of Gerasa (see Nelsen 1993, p. 71; Sangwin 2023; Sangwin & Tanswell 2023).

Figure 10 gives the base case and the first eight instances, but the claim is general for any odd number. Implicitly, the proof is by induction, and the diagram not only gives the base case, but shows the reader *how* an extra "layer" gets added to move from one case to the next, which is the inductive step. Reflecting on the procedure makes it obvious to the reader how the inductive step generalises for any *n*. My interpretation of how this proof works, then, is as a picture that first *demonstrates* the base case and then acts as a recipe for moving from one step to the next. It takes advantage of the ability

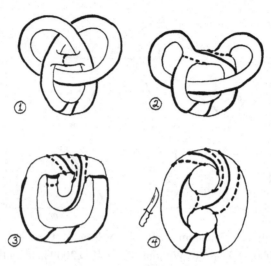

Figure 11 Using a knife to indicate proof actions (Rolfsen 1976, pp. 249–50; see
De Toffoli & Giardino 2015, p. 325). © Dale Rolfsen 1976.
Note: my thanks to Professor Rolfsen for permission to reproduce this image here.

of the readers to understand the procedure of adding the extra layers in order to
see how it will hold for any *n*.

Finally, consider the more advanced example from research-level mathematics explained by De Toffoli & Giardino (2015), who detail several proofs in
low-dimensional topology, and specifically one by Rolfsen (1976). The proof
involves a series of instructions for moving between a sequence of diagrams.
They summarise that: "We have to follow the instructions given in the text in
order to identify the various transitions connecting the pictures. For example, to
move from the fourth to the last picture, as the knife suggests, we cut the surface
open and lay it flat on the plane" (De Toffoli & Giardino 2015, p. 324).
(Figure 11).

These instructions explain various manipulations that are to be carried out
between the diagrams, such as "drilling holes", "inflating", "sewing" pieces
together, "cutting a surface open", and "flattening out". Indeed, one of the
pictures contains a picture of a knife to instruct the reader to make a cut in the
right place.

De Toffoli and Giardino argue that this proof is a hybrid of text and diagram
where neither part is dispensable: "Without the pictures, it would be impossible
to understand the text; conversely, without the text, it would be very hard to
correctly interpret the pictures: neither one is complete without the other. The
argument requires both for its cogency" (De Toffoli & Giardino 2015, p. 326).

As such, this example shows a recipe proof that requires both written instructions and the diagrammatic elements to interpret them. De Toffoli and Giardino discuss various features of this proof, such as the heterogeneous set of permissible actions, the way that the visual representations are used to trigger the "manipulative imagination", which combines the reader's cognitive and visual abilities to allow them to understand what actions can be rigorously carried out, and what their effect would be on the represented items.[47] However, for the purposes of the recipe model of proof, the simpler point is that this model is the most direct and faithful way to understand such a proof, which is clearly using instructions to guide a reader through a complicated and heterogeneous piece of reasoning.

5.4 Epistemology of Proofs

Let us turn now to the epistemology of proofs because this is another place where the recipe model offers a new proposal. Recall from Section 2.1 that one of the core reasons for being interested in rigorous proofs is their link to mathematical knowledge. The orthodox view is that one gains a priori mathematical knowledge from rigorous mathematical proofs. The very simplest picture of this would be that one starts by knowing the premises (or axioms) of a proof, and then carries out a priori-preserving inferences, whereby one derives further a priori knowledge of the theorem that has been proved.

The orthodox picture is highly idealised and immediate difficulties arise when one tries to apply it at a more real-world level. For one thing, the story is one of *gaining* mathematical knowledge, but a real mathematician might forget things again, over time. With the inherent complexity of mathematical arguments, it is not uncommon for a mathematician to forget the exact proof of some theorem, but also to be able to readily reconstruct it based on the main idea, or even to be able to reinvent it entirely, should the need arise. So, when exactly is a theorem still *known*?

Löwe and Müller (2008) address this question by looking through many options for making precise the conditions for having mathematical knowledge. They demonstrate that many of the intuitive options fail to accurately ascribe knowledge in even basic cases. For example, one proposal, that you have mathematical knowledge of a theorem when you have a proof available, falls

---

[47] In response to criticism by Tatton-Brown (2021), De Toffoli (2021b) elaborates on how these proofs can be considered rigorous even by the standard view, but maintains that the real object of investigation in De Toffoli and Giardino's (2015) study was acceptability criteria (i.e., the descriptive part of when mathematicians will actually accept a proof), which their study shows may depend on local criteria without, she argues, thereby implying that rigour is merely local or socially constructed.

down because "availability" is too broad: this option would say you could know a theorem merely by loading up the *ArXiv* containing a paper that proves it, or by stepping foot in the library. Another proposal would be that you have mathematical knowledge of a theorem if you are in principle able to generate a proof of it. Löwe and Müller point out that this would require further specifying what "in principle", "generate", and "proof" mean. For example, one could demand a formal proof, but then most mathematicians would be unable to produce this unless the "in principle" were very permissive (recall the hypothetical logician helper from Section 3.5), in which case it risks being too permissive and ascribing knowledge that the mathematician doesn't really possess. Regardless of how one fills these out, a general worry with this approach is that the modal component will always be too permissive, since the theorems that a mathematician could in principle generate proofs for will always outstrip those that they actually know. Löwe and Müller's solution is to argue that mathematical knowledge is context-dependent, since different contexts will prescribe different standards, and furthermore that it must invoke some notion of *mathematical skill*.[48] Their idea is that a mathematician's skills will be the deciding factor in whether a mathematician possesses some mathematical knowledge. For example, in a permissive context, knowing a proof idea might already be sufficient for knowledge, in which case a mathematician who is not an expert in that particular area can have sufficient skills to have mathematical knowledge. However, in a more demanding context, it may be that only the mathematical expert of some area, who has the skills necessary to set out the exact details of a proof, would count as knowing the proof.

Nonetheless, Löwe and Müller's (2008) proposal still seems open to the modal objection that a mathematician will often have the skills to prove more things than they actually know. One way out of this tangle is to expand our understanding of what kinds of knowledge proofs are important for. Rav (1999) famously argues that the substantial part of mathematical knowledge is not of the theorems that are proved, but of the proofs themselves:

> Proofs rather than the statement-form of theorems are the bearers of mathematical knowledge. Theorems are in a sense just tags, labels for proofs, summaries of information, headlines of news, editorial devices. The whole arsenal of mathematical methodologies, concepts, strategies and techniques

---

[48] They expand on this in a follow up paper (Löwe & Müller 2010), where they argue that the relevant skills are professional mathematical skills; those necessary for being a professional mathematician. They point out that some of these necessary skills may be peripheral (such as skill at booking trains to conferences), but that there will be no clear dividing line that forms an "epistemic core" of just those strictly necessary skills.

for solving problems, the establishment of interconnections between theories, the systematisation of results – *the entire mathematical know-how is embedded in proofs*. (Rav 1999, p. 20)

The point is that the focus on conditions for possessing a piece of propositional knowledge of some theorem statement is too narrow. Proofs provide knowledge of how something is proved, as well as a range of other types of knowledge. Here we can draw on the distinction introduced by Ryle (1946) between *knowledge-that* and *knowledge-how*. Knowledge-that is propositional knowledge: knowledge that some fact is true. Knowledge-how is practical knowledge: knowledge of how to do some action or activity. We can thus interpret Rav's proposal to include the idea that the knowledge-how in proofs is more important in mathematics than the knowledge-that of theorem statements.[49]

Using this distinction, a new proposal on mathematical knowledge can be put forward: that you know that a theorem is true when you know how to prove it. This is extremely close to Löwe and Müller's (2008, 2010) skill-based proposal, but does not suffer the same modal problem of including all the things they would hypothetically be able to prove. Indeed, knowledge-how is closely connected to skills, abilities, competences, and capacities that agents possess (see Hornsby 2012).

For this proposal to offer a useful insight into mathematical knowledge, it needs to give more detail about what mathematical knowledge-how is. This is a question the recipe model can help to answer. With the focus on proofs as recipes for certain kinds of mathematical activities, there is an immediate link to knowing how to carry out those activities. Furthermore, the recipe model also leads us to consider the kinds of actions that are undertaken, so in turn tells us the kind of actions that the mathematician needs to know how to do. We will dive deeper into this question in the next section.

5.5 What Kind of Actions?

An important question for the recipe model of proofs is: what kind of actions does proving involve? If a proof is merely a vehicle by which to record and communicate the knowledge of how to go about enacting some piece of mathematical reasoning, then we want to know about those actions and get a better understanding of what they are. In this section I will look at some of the

---

[49] For a more detailed dive into mathematical know-how, see Tanswell (2016b, ch. 4). The connection between mathematics and Ryle's knowledge-how was already drawn by Löwe and Müller (2010). From a different direction, Rodin's (2014) mathematical arguments also respond to this distinction between knowledge-how and knowledge-that.

existing proposals: that they are *speech acts*, *inferential actions*, or *epistemic actions*.

Ruffino, San Mauro, and Venturi (2021) argue that mathematical texts involve *speech acts*, in the tradition of Austin (1962). Even stronger, they argue that the pragmatics of the different speech acts are an essential part of mathematics. For example, to understand the difference between content tagged as 'Theorem', 'Lemma', 'Proposition', 'Fact', 'Observation', 'Corollary', and 'Claim', they argue that we need to see them as combining two kinds of speech acts. The first is as an *assertion* of the content, while the second is a *declarative* speech act that places the given assertion in a structural hierarchy of how the author perceives their role in the theory. Similarly, mathematical definitions are taken to be declarative speech acts, declaring that a certain term be used in a particular way. Ruffino et al. do not consider the internal workings of a proof, but it is clear that the same ideas would apply; that proofs contain some assertions, some declaratives (for instance, the inclusive imperatives we have discussed could be analysed in this way), and some directive imperatives (as we have seen in Section 5.2).

However, while Ruffino et al. (2021) make a convincing case that the pragmatics of speech acts are important to mathematics, it does not seem like this will suffice for all the actions a recipe proof can prescribe. For one thing, the speech acts seem to be primarily on the part of the author of a proof, but a recipe is directed at the reader. The author may assert some mathematical proposition, but the reader is instead asked to assent to it, based on the justification given in the proof, and then to enact it.[50]

Larvor (2012) instead makes the case that informal proofs are best understood as *systems of inferential actions*. He argues that speech acts are insufficient to capture the kind of actions that may be involved in a proof. His argument is that the inferential actions involved in proving can act on a diverse array of objects or no object at all:

> Sometimes, we act inferentially on non-propositional representations of the subject-matter such as diagrams, notational expressions, physical models, mental models and computer models. Sometimes, we re-describe the subject-matter in some insightful way, perhaps with the aid of an analogy or metaphor. ... Some inferential actions do not have objects; for example, one might show that an unlikely act (such as a new move in gymnastics) is possible by performing it. (Larvor 2012, p. 721)

---

[50] Perhaps one could explain this using the perlocutionary force of a speech act, that is, its effect on the audience. This is certainly an option worth exploring, but would not be sufficient to explain mathematical actions in proofs as solely a matter of speech acts.

These inferential actions thus include other possible action types beside speech acts. For example, recall from Section 5.3 De Toffoli and Giardino's (2015) examples involving the manipulative imagination acting on diagrams in low-dimensional topology. They explicitly draw on Larvor's work to classify these as instances of inferential actions, but it would not make sense to describe them as speech acts.

However, inferential actions might still not enumerate all of the action types that the recipe model of proof predicts the reader is instructed to carry out. As we saw, not all of the actions in a proof are strictly speaking inferential. Instructions can also tell the reader to construct new objects to work with, adopt new notations, take note of salient facts, or refer to previously established results.[51]

A way to broaden this is to consider the mathematical actions directed by proofs to include *epistemic actions*. This proposal is evaluated by Gelfert (2022) who draws on a classic distinction from philosophy of action between pragmatic actions and epistemic actions by Kirsh and Maglio (1994). Pragmatic actions are those that are immediately directed at some physical goal, for example, moving my legs in order to climb up a hill. Epistemic actions are those "physical actions that make mental computation easier, faster, or more reliable – [they] are external actions that an agent performs to change his or her own computational state" (Kirsh & Maglio 1994, p. 514). Unlike pragmatic actions, these might not directly pursue a defined goal, but instead help with the cognitive work required to achieve it. One can consider some of the examples we have already seen, such as using physical models or manipulating written notations (Gelfert's central example), as epistemic actions involved in proving. Gelfert also points to the use of gestures in presenting mathematics at the blackboard, such as that studied by Greiffenhagen and Sharrock (2005), as involving epistemic actions. He does, however, argue that the external, physical requirement on epistemic actions makes it hard to recycle this distinction properly into mathematics. For instance, manipulating diagrammatic representations cognitively (and so internally) would not fit exactly, despite seemingly taking on a similar enabling role for mental computation. One option is to drop the external, physical part of the definition of epistemic actions. Another option is to recognise parallel classes of actions, either internal or external, which play an enabling role within proofs. For example, it may be that introducing an additional

---

[51] This may be a merely terminological worry about calling them "inferential", since Larvor (2012) seems to cast the net wide for which things might be included. On a more permissive reading, the proposal to see proofs as systems of inferential actions is closely related to and directly inspired the recipe model. This relationship is explored by Tanswell (in press).

construction, diagram, or piece of notation within a proof is not strictly required for the argument, but does make understanding it significantly easier, thus enabling cognitive engagement.

Overall, it seems that the kinds of actions that a proof instructs its reader to carry out can vary dramatically. While some actions may be internal, cognitive ones, they might also be external and physically embodied. They must include a diverse array of inferential actions, but also other mathematical actions, like Rotman's inclusive instructions for establishing a shared domain of concepts, references, and notations. Mathematical actions might include speech acts of varying sorts, but can also include non-linguistic activity, such as using visual imagination to manipulate a cognitive representation.[52] The result of this section is therefore that there is no clear, uniform class of all mathematical actions, but that there is a great deal of potential for identifying interesting and important subclasses to analyse.

5.6 Rigorous Recipes

We can now consider what the recipe model will say about mathematical rigour. What makes a proof, seen as giving a recipe for mathematical actions, rigorous? The general answer is that following the recipe should lead you to establishing the theorem, just as following a cooking recipe should lead you to making the desired meal. Let us examine this in more detail.

First of all, a recipe comes with a list of ingredients. A proof will make use of certain definitions and rely on previously established results. Then, according to the recipe model, a *rigorous* proof will make such dependencies clear and explicit, as needed. Even stronger, one could enforce the norm that all of the previous results already need to be rigorously proved. However, I believe this would be too strong because even if a previous result has not been rigorously proved, so long as the dependency on the assumption is made explicit, the current proof may still be rigorous. This might point to a distinction between a rigorous proof and a rigorously established theorem, where the latter requires that all of its dependencies are rigorous.

Second, the proof must not contain any errors or gaps. As with other models of rigour, this should mean that no inferences are of a sort that can lead one into falsehoods. However, unlike the various versions of the standard view, the recipe model can only partially rely on formal logic to identify which inferences are acceptable. Additionally, it needs to give an account of which instructions are acceptable in a proof. Given the diverse array of actions that one can be told to undertake, as we saw in Section 5.5 , this task may be formidable.

---

[52] For example, recall Azzouni's inference packages from Section 3.6.

Nonetheless, formal logic does not have a monopoly on rigour. There are ways to approach the task of understanding how the various mathematical actions might be rigorously set out. For example, Larvor talks about inferential actions as requiring systems of control:

> [F]or every kind of inferential action, there must be a corresponding means of control, to ensure rigour. Sometimes these controls are simple rules like "do not divide by zero". In other cases, these controls may be the fruit of mathematical research (think of the seventeenth-century experiments in exponentiation, or the nineteenth-century developments necessary to establish rules for handling infinite series). (Larvor 2012, p. 728)

Developing a sense of what kind of actions are allowed under which circumstances, in the form of these controls, seems to be crucial in learning mathematics.

Of course, we have seen that not all actions in a proof are strictly inferential so assessing rigour will not always come down to checking for valid inferences. Other kinds of actions might be assessed in different ways. Taking the presence of instructions in proofs seriously, we can observe several ways that these might go wrong in a proof, where one cannot follow an instruction.[53] This might happen when the recipe instructs you to do something impossible, for example, "Multiply by the largest odd number." Alternatively, it may be that an instruction doesn't result in what it claims to – for example, "Factorise the equation to get . . .", where it does not factorise in the given way. Similarly, an instruction may tell us to use something that cannot be used in that way. These errors may well be subtle, such as when an instruction works for most cases but fails for difficult edge cases.

We can extend this thinking to gaps in a proof, since a rigorous proof should not contain gaps. A gap might occur in a proof on the recipe model when one can follow some instruction, but the proof doesn't justify why. Alternatively, there may be a gap if a proof leaves the reader unsure how to proceed, by failing to string instructions together into a coherent whole.[54]

---

[53] Here I am following a line of discussion from Weber and Tanswell (2022, sect. 5.1). There we focus on the educational importance of teaching students about the instructions found in proofs. Simply put: if we want students to be able to understand proofs as they are written, and they are written containing instructions, then it is better to conceive of proofs on the recipe model and teach students how to understand such instructions directly.

[54] A different approach to rigorous mathematical instructions is taken by Fine (2005) in his work on "procedural postulationism", where he attempts to build a foundational system for mathematics based on instructions. I have been describing what philosophy can say about the mathematical practice of having many different mathematical instructions. In contrast, Fine defines a set of logical, instructional rules that can be used to generate a menagerie of mathematical objects. The questions of rigour for Fine are different, for example, about whether the postulation rules can be consistently carried out.

This only gestures at a full account of rigorous recipes. If we want to account for rigour in actual practice, however, and real proofs involve these kinds of instructions, then it follows that it is necessary to pursue this project further.

5.7 Conclusion

To conclude this section on the recipe model of proofs, let us consider its strengths and weaknesses. The recipe model is closer to mathematical practice than the standard view, so has the advantage of explaining the descriptive, empirical facts more immediately. The linguistic data on the presence of imperatives in written mathematical proofs ties directly with seeing proofs as recording and communicating how to carry out the activity they describe. The recipe model predicts the use of imperatives and instructions, but can also accommodate instructions issued through diagrams. It also motivates a richer picture of mathematical knowledge, which has a clear role for non-propositional knowledge-how, so is good for investigating the epistemology of mathematics and how it links to proving. The emphasis on actions and activities also aligns nicely with the practical turn in philosophy of mathematics: interest in practices is, at least in part, interest in the actions and activities of mathematicians when doing mathematics.

The recipe model fits well with many of the empirical results we have already encountered. For example, the context-dependence of judgements about validity, acceptability, and what counts as proof (Weber 2008; Heinze 2010; Inglis & Alcock 2012; Inglis et al. 2013; Weber & Czocher 2019; Davies et al. 2021) would support the idea that what counts as a sufficient recipe for a piece of reasoning (or cooking a meal) will vary by target audience.

Furthermore, the empirical literature contrasts two pictures of how mathematicians read proofs: "zooming out" to understand the overall structure and "line-by-line checking" of the individual steps. In interview studies, mathematicians often describe using a "zooming out" approach (Weber 2008; Mejía-Ramos & Weber 2014), but eye-tracking studies seem to indicate that mathematicians generally just use "line-by-line checking" (Inglis & Alcock 2012; Panse et al. 2018). Nonetheless, Andersen's (2017) interview study about the mathematics refereeing process saw her interviewees reporting that they would employ the "zooming out" process, only checking the details of proofs or subproofs for results that "stand out as surprising or suspicious" (Andersen 2017, p. 186). Such an approach would rely on their expertise in having a feel for what results are surprising or suspicious – for example, by knowing how strong certain assumptions normally need to be to deliver certain kinds of results. Again, the recipe model can account for this well. Sometimes the best way to get the big picture of a recipe is to zoom out to the overall picture, looking for the most important instructions or clusters of instructions. Sometimes, though, line-by-line examination might be the best way to understand what the overall strategy being deployed is. The model can also explain that mathematicians might have sufficient experience to be able to tell quickly which instructions need to be checked carefully, because they are difficult, error-prone, or otherwise suspicious, just as a chef can pick out which bits of a recipe will be the most difficult or error-prone to make.

The recipe model does not match well with descriptive–normative descriptions of what mathematicians say counts as a proof, since these tend to focus on formalistic ideas better captured by the standard view (see Müller-Hill 2009; Davies et al. 2020). By moving away from the standard views, the recipe model is less favourable for projects that rely on identifying rigour and formality, such as in metamathematics or the formalisation of mathematics for computer-checkability. By embracing actions, instructions, and non-propositional practical knowledge, the resulting account of rigour will have to address a diverse array of action types, which, as we have seen, involves some complexity. I would argue, though, that this diversity is a fact about proving as it is found in practice, and that it is crucial to work to explain it.

6 Rigour Is a Virtue

6.1 Introduction

Consider the difference between the description of a "long proof" and that of a "creative proof". In the first case, it is unambiguous that "long" is a property of the proof presentation. There may still be contextual factors that affect what counts as a long proof: the standards for a long proof in a school classroom may be different to those for a long proof for a research mathematics journal, just as the standards for "heavy" will be different for new-born babies and sumo wrestlers. In the case of "creative proof", however, the proof presentation itself isn't necessarily creative, but rather displays the creativity of the proof's author, who has come up with creative ideas.[55] A proof itself doesn't have the imaginative and original ideas characteristic of creativity, but instead is labelled as "creative" when it takes an approach that shows those creative characteristics on the part of the originator of the proof. In this case, creativity is primarily an *intellectual virtue* of the prover, and only secondarily a property of the proof.[56]

---

[55] To be clear, proof presentations can also be creative, as is exemplified brilliantly by Ording (2019).

[56] Once one starts to pay attention to this distinction, it turns out that dividing commonly used adjectives for proofs between the two categories is surprisingly hard. For example, is a "dull

In all of the models of proof and rigour we have seen so far, "rigorous" is treated as a mere property of proofs, just like "long".[57] In this section, I will consider the *virtue model of rigour* that emerges when one instead treats rigour as primarily an intellectual virtue of the mathematician engaged in proving activities. This builds on recent work by various scholars who have proposed adopting some of the ideas from virtue theory for the philosophy of mathematics (Tanswell 2016b; Su 2017, 2020; Aberdein et al. 2021; Ernest 2021; Martin 2021; Morris 2021; Rittberg 2021; Tanswell & Kidd 2021).

Before we get started on this model, let us consider a small piece of empirical motivation for this view. In their study of mathematical beauty, Inglis and Aberdein (2015) investigated 80 adjectives that mathematicians could apply to proofs, asking them how well each one applied to a proof of their participants' own choosing. Using the responses from 255 mathematicians, their results revealed clusters of these adjectives into four "dimensions": *aesthetics* (relating to mathematical beauty); *utility* (relating to how useful the proof is); *precision* (how precise the proof is); and *intricacy* (how simple or complicated the proof is). For example, the aesthetics dimension contained adjectives like "beautiful", "profound", "charming", "deep", and "elegant". Importantly, the adjective "rigorous" was on the *precision* dimension, alongside "precise", "meticulous", "careful", "accurate", "clear", "definitive", and "unambiguous". The adjectives "meticulous" and "careful" are obvious candidates for being primarily about the intellectual virtues of the mathematician, manifested in the proof they have come up with, rather than a direct description of the proof itself. The guiding thought in this section is to take "rigorous" to be of the same kind.

6.2 Mathematical Epistemic Virtues

The central proposal of the virtue model of rigour is to draw on the tools of virtue theory in studying rigour. The modern approach to virtue ethics was championed by authors such as Anscombe (1958), Foot (1978), and MacIntyre (1985), who all followed a broadly neo-Aristotelean stance (Aristotle 2009), though virtue theory is also found in Confucian, Buddhist, and Hindu traditions (see Hursthouse & Pettigrove 2022). The guiding thought is to look at moral character as the central pillar of ethical theory, rather than deontology or

---

proof" one that is totally routine with too much calculation, or is it one that lacks interesting or creative ideas? One adjective that has received quite some attention in the literature is "explanatory". The difference between explanatoriness as merely a property of proofs or as something connected to the agent's understanding is present in the literature as Delarivière et al.'s (2017) distinction between *ontic* and *epistemic* explanation. Taking this even further, it may well be that many adjectives linked to proofs have these two different senses.

[57] The difficulty of separating properties of the product from properties of the agent is discussed by Tanswell and Kidd (2021, p. 417).

consequentialism. Extending this idea, virtue epistemologists emphasise the importance of one's intellectual character in the pursuit of knowledge. This approach has two broad camps: the virtue reliabilists and virtue responsibilists. The reliabilists generally take the relevant virtues to be stable, reliable abilities (Greco 2010), or competences (Sosa 2009). The responsibilists take virtues to be excellent intellectual character traits (Code 1987; Montmarquet 1993; Zagzebski 1996). In the recent literature, various hybrid options are also available (Battaly 2008; Ohlhorst 2022).

Whichever account of intellectual virtues one prefers, they will both agree that intellectual virtues are manifested in certain kinds of activities. Therefore, we will be interested in intellectual virtues that play a role in mathematical activities. In keeping with the rest of this Element, we can focus this discussion specifically on proofs and proving, but this is not as necessary for the virtue model of rigour. One advantage of taking rigour to be associated with the mathematicians themselves is that this provides a uniform account of rigour across different kinds of mathematical activities. After all, one can approach any area of mathematics or mathematical activity in a rigorous way, not just those that involve proving.

Nonetheless, let us investigate what the virtue model will say about rigour in proving. The main idea will be that rigorous proving is rigorous just because it manifests the intellectual virtue of rigour, which involves meticulous and careful attention to detail. On a reliabilist account, this will be further filled out in terms of competences or abilities, that is, meticulousness is about being able to spot and correct gaps and errors reliably. On a responsibilist account, this will be about stable traits of character, that is, the mathematician will develop habits of care and attention in their work that guard against gaps and errors.

One thing that virtue models of rigour will give us is a solution to a persistent epistemic puzzle. We have seen in other models that mathematical knowledge from proofs has inherited the challenge from epistemology of explaining what it means to justify our beliefs "in the right way". (This emerged in both the standard view about justifying the belief that a formal proof is available, and in the recipe model of having activities carried out in the right way.) Crucially, however detailed a given proof is, one does not gain knowledge from it unless one engages with it in the right way: for example, making the correct inferences at the right points. In epistemic terms, this is about avoiding epistemic luck, where incorrect reasoning happens to lead to the correct result by coincidence.[58]

---

[58] Some cases might involve subtle errors, while others might be what Aberdein (2010) calls "howlers", illustrated by this humorous example from Maxwell (1959, p. 88):
"To solve the equation $(x + 3)(2 - x) = 4$. Either $x + 3 = 4$ so $x = 1$. Or $2 - x = 4$ so $x = -2$. Correct."

For instance, someone who reads through a proof, but misunderstands why the inferences succeed at each step, cannot truly be said to know the theorem proved. The virtue model of rigour can answer this puzzle because the missing ingredient seems to be outside of the proof, and to do with how the agent carries out their reasoning. For the virtue model the answer is that "the right way" of doing the reasoning is to do so rigorously, deploying intellectual character traits to successfully gain knowledge.

Perhaps the easiest way to see this is using Sosa's "triple A" account about *accuracy, adroitness*, and *aptness* (Sosa 2009). In Sosa's famous archery example, when an archer hits the target, the shot was *accurate*. But one can be accurate because of a lucky shot. Another evaluative dimension is how skilful a shot was, its *adroitness*. However, an adroit shot may not be accurate if a sudden gust of wind redirects the arrow after it has been released. Furthermore, an adroit and accurate shot might still be missing something: in the "lucky" case where one gust of wind redirects the arrow, then a second one directs it back. Sosa proposes that the evaluative component necessary for knowledge is *aptness*: that the shot is accurate because it is adroit, that is, that the manifestation of the competence is the reason for the accuracy. For knowledge, one's beliefs must be accurate because they manifest the intellectual virtues. Applied to the case of mathematical knowledge, one's mathematical beliefs must be apt, meaning they are accurate because they are adroit, and so they must be true because one has manifested the intellectual virtue of rigour.

Using this virtue model of rigour, it is also possible to explain some of the empirical findings we have discussed. One of the main results of the literature is the context-dependence of judgements of rigour: for example, what is suitable for a student is not always suitable for a mathematics journal and vice versa. The explanation for this would be simple: that proofs are written to cater to different levels of competence. When one can assume the reader will have a high level of mathematical competence, less needs to be communicated, whereas when one is teaching or assessing the level of competence of a proof, more needs to be made explicit to show that the proof has been adeptly written.

Additionally, Weber et al. (2022) have recently produced a clever study that examined how 16 senior maths PhD students gain certainty from proofs. They provided participants, sequentially, with a theorem statement that an infinite sum was equal to π; a proof for the claim; empirical evidence in the form of an Excel file demonstrating that the sum approached π rapidly; and finally, a copy of *The American Mathematical Monthly* from 1997 that contains a published version of the proof. At each step, they asked participants to rate how confident they are in the claim, with the results shown in Table 2.

Table 2 Results from Weber et al.'s (2022, p. 72) study of PhD students' confidence in a mathematical claim when given successive pieces of evidence.

Phase of the study	Average Confidence Score	# Participants who gained confidence	# Participants who were certain (score of 100)	# Participants with a score of 99 or higher	# Participants with a score of 95 or higher
After reading the claim	44.7	n/a	0	0	0
After reading the proof	82.4	15 (out of 16)	2	4	7
After reading empirical evidence	95.3	12 (out of 14)	6	7	13
After seeing the article	98.7	9 (out of 10)	8	12	16

It is striking that a relatively straightforward and rigorous proof leaves the participants with only 82 per cent average confidence, and that this further increases with appeals to empirical evidence and the authority of it being published. The mathematicians are also reluctant to say they are certain, rather than having a high confidence, suggesting an awareness of their own fallibility. One interesting point that arose in interviewing participants after the test was about the interaction between the proof and empirical evidence. Describing why they increased their confidence in light of the empirical evidence, one participant said: "[I may have] missed a log 2 along the way where everything seems to cancel out and the answer's not π. It's a lot harder to do that and have the sum converge to quite close to π, if not π" (Weber et al. 2022, p. 73).

This provides the valuable insight that even when we acknowledge the human fallibility inevitably present when reading and evaluating proofs, careful checking may nonetheless limit the space for possible errors. The quote here points out that the kind of minor errors that someone might miss in reading a proof, such as manipulation errors, are not compatible with getting the convergence correct. Coordinating a rigorous proof with other forms of evidence thus has the power to increase our confidence that no such error is present. Such empirical results can easily be explained by the virtue model: that the rigorous mathematician would be both careful not to be overconfident and sensitive to multiple sources of evidence. For the virtue theorist, rigour is not about deductive rigour attached to the proof itself, but about how mathematicians approach mathematics, so evidence about what doing careful, meticulous mathematics might look like in practice is very welcome.

Another advantage of the virtue model of rigour is that it broadens the scope of philosophy of mathematics because rigour is just one among many relevant intellectual virtues for mathematics. For example, recent research has already engaged with intellectual generosity (Morris 2021) and intellectual humility (Rittberg 2021). Francis Su (2017) argues for the importance to mathematics of virtues including *hopefulness*, *perseverance*, *joy* ("the wonder or awe or delight in the beauty of the created order", p. 486), *transcendence* ("the ability to embrace the mystery of it all", p. 486), *rigorous thinking*, *humility*, and *circumspection* ("we know the limits of our arguments, and we don't over-generalize", p. 488). Martin (2021) argues that with the increase in collaborative mathematics, there should be a new emphasis on social virtues that aid collaboration. Tanswell and Kidd (2021) weigh up the trade-offs between individual-level and collective virtues and vices in mathematics. All this opens up a lot of fertile, new material for philosophers of mathematical practice to investigate in the future.

6.3 Rigour and Justice

The virtue model of rigour also reveals another overlooked feature of rigour in mathematical practice. Describing a proof as "rigorous" may implicitly be used to make a judgement about the mathematicians who created it. Whenever one finds evaluative judgements of people, there will be the possibility that those judgements are made unfairly. Mathematics is no exception. As a discipline, it contains power dynamics, and plenty of opportunities for judgements about "rigour" to make a difference to who can participate, who gets jobs and material benefits, who wins prizes and accolades, whose ideas are respected and celebrated, and who has access to the mathematics community. When those judgements are made unfairly, the social structuring of the discipline reflects this disparity.

One infamous case where the meaning of "rigour" was central to a disagreement about mathematical practice was in the Jaffe–Quinn debate, triggered by a provocative article by Jaffe and Quinn (1993), with a selection of responses by Atiyah et al. (1994) and Thurston (1994).[59] Jaffe and Quinn's main argument was that the high standards of rigour for mathematical publication were being undermined by what they called "speculative mathematics", especially by work in mathematical physics. They argued that many results were being published in mathematics without actually being rigorously established, and that this has a series of negative effects on the state of mathematical knowledge. For example, the literature becomes unreliable and misleading; further work is discouraged because the credit for the results has already been claimed; areas of mathematics are deserted; and credit is unfairly claimed (Jaffe & Quinn 1993, p. 9). Various working mathematicians are even mentioned by name as having produced unrigorous mathematics. While ostensibly the argument is about mathematical rigour, it is clear that these issues are inseparable from social issues of disciplinary boundaries, inclusion and exclusion, and the fair distribution of credit.

The term *epistemic injustice* is used for cases where an injustice occurs in the setting of knowledge-making activities, such as mathematics. This notion was developed by Fricker (2007) who gave a framework for understanding injustices involving, for example, not sufficiently trusting testimony from marginalised groups, or depriving groups of conceptual resources for making sense of unfair practices.[60] In my own work and that of my collaborators (Rittberg et al. 2020; Tanswell & Rittberg 2020; Hunsicker & Rittberg 2022) we have explored some ways in which epistemic injustice can come about in mathematics, too.

---

[59] A detailed discussion of the cultural impact of Thurston's article is given by Hanna and Larvor (2020).

[60] It is worth noting that Fricker's work is also based in the virtue epistemology tradition, arguing that we need to develop the intellectual virtue of *epistemic justice*.

For example, we argued that judgements about the "novelty" of a piece of mathematics might seem like a straightforward matter (has it been published before or not?), but in fact judgements of novelty can lead to unjust exclusionary effects. What is considered known to the inner members of the mathematical community, who communicate at conferences and seminars, over dinner and drinks, by email or video calls, and so on is very different to what someone external to the mathematical community can consider known. Some people outside of the in-crowd must rely on publicly available resources such as online preprints, and navigating the literature via bibliographic references, libraries, and online search tools. This leads to what Hookway (2010) characterises as *participatory* epistemic injustices: it is harder for the outsiders to access the insiders' ideas of novelty, and this in turn decides who gets to participate in mathematical practices. Mathematics is a field that has a poor track record of diversity (see Hunsicker & Rittberg 2022, sect. 3), so structural barriers that exclude and disadvantage outsiders will often involve epistemic injustice (though not always, see Rittberg 2023).

Judgements of "rigour" can similarly function to include or exclude participants from mathematical communities. With the standard view discussed in Section 3 tracking what many mathematicians think are the standards of mathematics – that is, the standard view as a main part of the descriptive–normative view of rigour for many mathematicians – one might expect judgements of rigour to be objective. Either a proof is rigorous because it corresponds to a formal proof, or it isn't because it doesn't. However, like judgements of novelty, judgements of rigour may well be not so objective after all. We have already seen the empirical evidence that there can be substantial disagreements about valid proofs and acceptable gaps, cemented further in the work of Inglis and Aberdein (2016) who find widespread disagreement in mathematicians' judgements about the aesthetics, intricacy, utility, and precision of a given proof. Even if the standard view were correct about the normative standards, it is not necessarily correct about the descriptive question of understanding how judgements are actually made. Furthermore, we saw the mixed evidence on mathematical peer review: that many editors don't expect referees to check the proofs and that referees often only carefully examine proofs that "stand out as surprising or suspicious" (Andersen 2017, p. 186). Such judgements are clearly open to subjectivity. Therefore, we should also expect that judgements of rigour will not always be fair and just. This could manifest itself in marginalised groups being subjected to more strenuous demands to get their work published. There is evidence of this in the underrepresentation of women in prestigious mathematics journals (Mihaljević et al. 2016; Mihaljević & Santamaría 2022) and this parallels the same problem in the neighbouring field of economics, where women are held to higher standards (Hengel 2022). Not only does this demand more work to begin with, it also has cascading consequences for the opportunities a mathematician will have in their career, and ultimately whether they will have a career at all.

6.4 Conclusion

The virtue model of rigour is unlike the other models we have seen, because it changes the very object of investigation. It is no longer the proof itself that is rigorous, or not, but the mathematicians who are doing mathematics. Rather than looking at the reasoning encoded by a proof, the virtue model is interested in the evaluation of how the mathematician carries out that reasoning, and what kind of traits allow them to do well at it. For strengths, we have seen that the virtue model can draw on a major theory in modern epistemology to solve epistemic puzzles for proof and rigour, and that it provides a rich theory of other intellectual virtues relevant to mathematical practice. It is also a particularly helpful model for considering ways in which using judgements of rigour to make judgements about mathematicians might be unfair or unjust.

Turning to weaknesses of the virtue model of rigour: it is clear that the term "rigorous" is commonly applied to proofs even when the author is unknown. By moving away from the connection to the logic of mathematical inferences, the virtue model also attempts to explain different features of mathematical practice. Just as the proponent of the virtue model can point to these features of mathematics as having been overlooked by the other models, its critics can point to the logical structure of proofs as being largely ignored by the virtue model.

Another weakness is that the normative guidance the virtue model provides is less exact than, for example, a criterion of formalisability. Virtue theory is a normative theory (as seen in ethics and epistemology) but the guidance it provides is to cultivate certain ways of approaching mathematics and to have certain virtuous attitudes and behaviours. This may be less than helpful in the moment one has to evaluate a borderline case of a proof. However, it might also explain some of the contextual effects regarding how mathematicians judge proofs and rigour differently in different contexts, especially with respect to students' proofs. It may be that they are implicitly trying to evaluate how well the student has adopted the mathematical virtues that are being taught.

7 Conclusion

We have seen a selection of models of rigour and informal proofs, grouped into four families: the standard views; the argumentation and dialogical models; the recipe model of proofs; and virtue-theoretic models of rigour. A question that remains is: are these all of the options? One place we could look for inspiration for other models is in other metaphors for proof that have been used, such as proof as mountaineering (Hardy 1929), proof as exploring (Ryle 1971), proof as narrative (Thomas 2007), proofs as judicial reasoning (Thomas 2015; Termini 2019), proof as landscape gardening (Thomas 2017), proof as play (Su 2017), proof as journeying (Lane et al. 2019), proof as craft (Lane et al. 2019), and many more. Invoked as metaphors, these are all intended to emphasise and explain aspects of mathematical proofs in practice, but they have the potential to be developed into fully fledged conceptual models of proof and rigour.

I also haven't considered the model of informal rigour proposed by Kreisel (1967), and later developed by Isaacson (2011), Barton (2012), and Dean and Kurokawa (in press). Kreisel's notion is foremost about the rigorous use of concepts in mathematics, and how these progressively develop from intuitive notions to more robustly mathematical concepts amenable to axiomatisation, though informal rigour can also be applied to mathematical arguments, as Dean and Kurokawa argue. Relatedly, there is the possibility of a semantic model of rigour and informal proof, such as Leitgeb (2009) reads into the work of Gödel, and which is explicit in the work of Rav (1999). Both of these models are already further developed than those based on analogies and are clearly worth closer attention in future work.

I hope that in the process of describing and evaluating these models of rigour and proof, I have also implicitly made a case for *rigour pluralism*. None of the views we have seen is a uniquely correct account of the complicated tangle of normative and descriptive features of rigour and proofs in practice, and I think the quest to find such an account that underpins all of the functions and features of rigour is futile. Switching to a modelling perspective, however, allows us to observe that all of the models provide insights and explanations of different features of mathematics. Such a move makes it possible to say that the standard view, for example, is actually a very good model of rigour, despite the many criticisms showing that it isn't correct in some unqualified or objective way. The standard view models many mathematical proofs using the tools of formal logic, thereby enabling metamathematics, reverse mathematics, and computer verification to be done. That's fantastic! But it also makes it possible to recognise that other models might simply be better at accounting for some parts of mathematical practices, and in this Element we have seen many ways in which this is the case.

One final observation is that models are primarily representational, but they can also affect and shape the practices and the conceptions we have of them. The ubiquity of versions of the standard view in undergraduate mathematics teaching does have an impact on what mathematicians believe they are doing, which affects what they actually do. By illustrating other good models of rigour, I hope that these will in turn affect the way in which mathematics is really practiced.

In conclusion, if one is searching for the "true essence" of mathematical proofs, then a well-placed criticism can be devastating for the account. However, on the pluralistic approach, criticisms just reveal places where the model is a less good fit or can even be seen as harmless artefacts of the model. When dealing with conceptual models, it is important to keep in mind the difference between the model and the phenomena itself, and the ways in which some features of the model are just artefacts of the process of abstraction, idealisation, and formalisation. I thus hope to have convinced you that *rigour pluralism*, where there are many good models of rigour and informal proof, is a better approach than taking one account to give the ultimate correct answer.

References

Aberdein, A. (2005). The uses of argument in mathematics. *Argumentation*, 19, 287–301.

Aberdein, A. (2006). Managing informal mathematical knowledge: Techniques from informal logic. In Borwein, J. M., & Farmer, W. M. (eds.), *MKM 2006, Lecture Notes in Computer Science 4108* (pp. 208–21). Berlin, Springer.

Aberdein, A. (2007). The informal logic of mathematical proof. In Van Kerkhove, B., & Van Bendegem, J. P. (eds.), *Perspectives on Mathematical Practices* (pp. 135–51). Dordrecht, Springer.

Aberdein, A. (2010). Observations on sick mathematics. In Van Kerkhove, B., Van Bendegem, J. P., & de Vuyst, J. (eds.), *Philosophical Perspectives on Mathematical Practice* (pp. 269–300). Suwanee, GA, College Publications.

Aberdein, A. (2013). The parallel structure of mathematical reasoning. In Aberdein, A., & Dove, I. (eds.), *The Argument of Mathematics* (pp. 361–80). Dordrecht, Springer.

Aberdein, A. (2021). Dialogue types, argumentation schemes, and mathematical practice: Douglas Walton and mathematics. *Journal of Applied Logics*, 8(1), 159–82.

Aberdein, A. (2023). Deep disagreement in mathematics. *Global Philosophy*, *33*(1), 17.

Aberdein, A., Rittberg, C. J., & Tanswell, F. S. (2021). Virtue theory of mathematical practices: An introduction. *Synthese*, 199, 10167–80.

Alcolea Banegas, J. (1997). L'argumentació en matemàtiques. In Casaban i Moya, E. (ed.), *XIIè Congrés Valencià de Filosofia, València* (pp. 135–47). English translation (2013). Argumentation in mathematics. In Aberdein, A., & Dove, I. (eds.), *The Argument of Mathematics* (pp. 47–60). Dordrecht, Springer.

Andersen, L. E. (2017). On the nature and role of peer review in mathematics. *Accountability in Research*, 24(3), 177–92.

Andreatta, M., Bezdek, A., & Boronski, J. P. (2011). The problem of Malfatti: Two centuries of debate. *The Mathematical Intelligencer*, 33(1), 72–6.

Anscombe, G. E. M. (1958). Modern moral philosophy. *Philosophy*, 33(124), 1–19.

Antonutti Marfori, M. (2010). Informal proofs and mathematical rigour. *Studia Logica*, 96(2), 261–72.

Appel, K., & Haken, W. (1977). Every planar map is 4-colorable. Part I: Discharging. *Illinois Journal of Mathematics*, 21(3), 429–90.

Appel, K., Haken, W., & Koch, J. (1977). Every planar map is four colorable. Part II: Reducibility. *Illinois Journal of Mathematics*, 21(3), 491–567.

Aristotle. (2009). *The Nicomachean Ethics*. Ross, W. D. (trans.), 2nd edition revised and with notes by Brown, L. Oxford, Oxford University Press.

Atiyah, M., Borel, A., Chaitin, G. J. et al. (1994). Responses to: A. Jaffe and F. Quinn, 'Theoretical mathematics: Toward a cultural synthesis of mathematics and theoretical physics'. *Bulletin of the American Mathematical Society*, 30(2), 178–207.

Auslander, J. (2009). On the roles of proof in mathematics. In Gold, B., & Simons, R. A. (eds.), *Proof and Other Dilemmas: Mathematics and Philosophy* (pp. 61–78). Washington, DC, The Mathematical Association of America.

Austin, J. L. (1962). *How to Do Things with Words*. Oxford, Oxford University Press.

Avigad, J. (2021). Reliability of mathematical inference. *Synthese*, 198(8), 7377–99.

Azzouni, J. (2004). The derivation-indicator view of mathematical practice. *Philosophia Mathematica (III)*, 12(2), 81–106.

Azzouni, J. (2005). Is there still a sense in which mathematics can have foundations. In Sica, G. (ed.), *Essays on the Foundations of Mathematics and Logic* (pp. 9–48). Monza, Polimetrica.

Azzouni, J. (2009). Why do informal proofs conform to formal norms? *Foundations of Science*, 14(1), 9–26.

Azzouni, J. (2020). The algorithmic-device view of informal rigorous mathematical proof. In Sriraman, B. (ed.), *Handbook of the History and Philosophy of Mathematical Practice* (pp. 1–82). Cham, Springer. https://doi.org/10.1007/978-3-030-19071-2_4-1.

Barany, M. J. (2011). God, king, and geometry: Revisiting the introduction to Cauchy's Cours d'analyse. *Historia Mathematica*, 38(3), 368–88.

Barany, M. J. (2013). Stuck in the middle: Cauchy's Intermediate Value Theorem and the history of analytic rigor. *Notices of the AMS*, 60(10), 1334–8.

Barany, M. J. (2020). Impersonation and personification in mid-twentieth century mathematics. *History of Science*, 58(4), 417–36.

Barton, N. (2012). Structural relativity and informal rigour. In Oliveri, G., Ternullo, C., & Boscolo, S. (eds.), *Objects, Structures, and Logics: FilMat Studies in the Philosophy of Mathematics* (pp. 133–74). Cham, Springer.

Bass, H. (2003). The Carnegie Initiative on the Doctorate: The case of mathematics. *Notices of the AMS*, 50(7), 767–76.

Battaly, H. (2008). Virtue epistemology. *Philosophy Compass*, 3(4), 639–63.

Beall, J. (1999). From full blooded Platonism to really full blooded Platonism. *Philosophia Mathematica (III)*, 7(3), 322–5.

Beall, J. C., & Restall, G. (2005). *Logical Pluralism*. Oxford, Oxford University Press.

Blåsjö, V. (2022). Operationalism: An interpretation of the philosophy of ancient Greek geometry. *Foundations of Science*, 27(2), 587–708.

Bourbaki, N. (1968). *Elements of Mathematics, Theory of Sets*. Reading, MA, Addison-Wesley.

Brown J. (1999). *Philosophy of Mathematics: An Introduction to the World of Proofs and Pictures*. London, Routledge.

Buldt, B., Löwe, B., & Müller, T. (2008). Towards a new epistemology of mathematics. *Erkenntnis*, 68(3), 309–29.

Burgess, J. P. (2015). *Rigor and Structure*. Oxford, Oxford University Press.

Burgess, J., & De Toffoli, S. (2022). What is mathematical rigor? *Aphex*, 25, 1–17.

Cantù, P., & Luciano, E. (2021). Giuseppe Peano and his school: Axiomatics, symbolism and rigor. *Philosophia Scientiæ. Travaux d'histoire et de philosophie des sciences*, 25(1), 3–14.

Carter, J. (2019). Philosophy of mathematical practice: Motivations, themes and prospects. *Philosophia Mathematica (III)*, 27(1), 1–32.

Cellucci, C. (2018). Definition in mathematics. *European Journal for Philosophy of Science*, 8(3), 605–29.

Code, L. (1987). *Epistemic Responsibility*. Hanover, NH, University Press of New England.

Cook, R. T. (2000). *Logic-as-Modeling: A New Perspective on Formalization*. Doctoral dissertation, The Ohio State University. https://etd.ohiolink.edu/acprod/odb_etd/etd/r/1501/10?clear=10&p10_accession_num=osu1260202088.

Cook, R. T. (2010). Let a thousand flowers bloom: A tour of logical pluralism. *Philosophy Compass*, 5(6), 492–504.

Cotnoir, A. J. (2018). Logical nihilism. In Wyatt, J., Pedersen, N. J. L. L., & Kellen, N. (eds.), *Pluralisms in Truth and Logic* (pp. 301–29). Cham, Palgrave Macmillan.

Coumans, V. J. W. (2021). Definitions (and concepts) in mathematical practice. In Sriraman, B. (ed.), *Handbook of the History and Philosophy of Mathematical Practice* (n. pag.). Cham, Springer. https://doi.org/10.1007/978-3-030-19071-2_94-1.

Coumans, V. J. W., & Consoli, L. (2023). Definitions in practice: An interview study. *Synthese*, 202(23), 1–32.

Davies, B., Alcock, L., & Jones, I. (2020). Comparative judgement, proof summaries and proof comprehension. *Educational Studies in Mathematics*, 105(2), 181–97.

Davies, B., Alcock, L., & Jones, I. (2021). What do mathematicians mean by proof? A comparative-judgement study of students' and mathematicians' views. *The Journal of Mathematical Behavior*, 61, 100824.

Davies, B., Miller, D., & Infante, N. (2021). The role of authorial context in mathematicians' evaluations of proof. *International Journal of Mathematical Education in Science and Technology*, 54(5), 725–39.

De Morgan, A. (1838). Mathematical induction. *The Penny Cyclopedia*, 12, 465–6.

De Toffoli, S. (2021a). Groundwork for a fallibilist account of mathematics. *The Philosophical Quarterly*, 71(4), 1–22.

De Toffoli, S. (2021b). Reconciling rigour and intuition. *Erkenntnis*, 86, 1783–802.

De Toffoli, S. (2023). Who's afraid of mathematical diagrams? *Philosophers' Imprint*, 23, 9. https://doi.org/10.3998/phimp.1348.

De Toffoli, S., & Fontanari, C. (2022). Objectivity and rigor in classical Italian algebraic geometry. *Noesis: Objectivity in Mathematics*, 38, 195–212.

De Toffoli, S., & Fontanari, C. (2023). Recalcitrant disagreement in mathematics: An 'endless and depressing controversy' in the history of Italian algebraic geometry. *Global Philosophy*, 33(4), 1–29.

De Toffoli, S., & Giardino, V. (2015). An inquiry into the practice of proving in low-dimensional topology. In Lolli, G., Panza, M., & Venturi, G. (eds.), *From Logic to Practice* (pp. 315–36). Cham, Springer.

Dean, W., & Kurokawa, H. (in press). On the methodology of informal rigour: Set theory, semantics, and intuitionism. In Antonutti Marfori, M., & Petrolo, M. (eds.), *Intuitionism, Computation, and Proof: Selected Themes from the Research of G. Kreisel*, Springer.

Delarivière, S., Frans, J., & Van Kerkhove, B. (2017). Mathematical explanation: A contextual approach. *Journal of Indian Council of Philosophical Research*, 34(2), 309–29.

Detlefsen, M. (2009). Proof: Its nature and significance. In Gold, B., & Simons, R. A. (eds.), *Proof and Other Dilemmas: Mathematics and Philosophy* (pp. 3–32). Washington, DC, The Mathematical Association of America.

Dove, I. J. (2013). Towards a theory of mathematical argument. In Aberdein, A., & Dove, I. (eds.), *The Argument of Mathematics* (pp. 291–308). Springer, Dordrecht.

Dutilh Novaes, C. (2011). The different ways in which logic is (said to be) formal. *History and Philosophy of Logic*, 32(4), 303–32.

Dutilh Novaes, C. (2021). *The Dialogical Roots of Deduction: Historical, Cognitive, and Philosophical Perspectives on Reasoning*. Cambridge, Cambridge University Press.

Ernest, P. (1998). *Social Constructivism as a Philosophy of Mathematics.* Albany, NY, State University of New York Press.

Ernest, P. (2021). Mathematics, ethics and purism: An application of MacIntyre's virtue theory. *Synthese,* 199(1), 3137–67.

Eves, H. (1965). *A Survey of Geometry, Volume 2.* Boston, MA, Allyn and Bacon.

Ferreirós, J. (2008). The crisis in the foundations of mathematics. In Gowers, T., Barrow-Green, & Leader, I. (eds.), *The Princeton Companion to Mathematics* (pp. 142–56). Princeton, NJ, Princeton University Press.

Fine, K. (2005). Our knowledge of mathematical objects. In Gendler T. S., & Hawthorne, J. (eds.), *Oxford Studies in Epistemology* (pp. 89–109). Oxford, Oxford Academic.

Foot, P. (1978,) *Virtues and Vices and Other Essays in Moral Philosophy.* Oxford: Blackwell.

Franks, Curtis (2015). Logical nihilism. In Hirvonen, Å., Kontinen, J., Kossak, R., & Villaveces, A. (eds.), *Logic without Borders: Essays on Set Theory, Model Theory, Philosophical Logic and Philosophy of Mathematics,* pp. 147–66. Berlin, De Gruyter.

Frege, G. (1884) *The Foundations of Arithmetic.* Austin, J. L. (trans.), 1953. Oxford, Blackwell.

Fricker, M. (2007). *Epistemic Injustice: Power and the Ethics of Knowing.* Oxford, Oxford University Press.

Geist, C., Löwe, B., & Kerkhove, B. V. (2010). Peer review and knowledge by testimony in mathematics. In Löwe, B., & Müller, T. (eds.), *Philosophy of Mathematics: Sociological Aspects and Mathematical Practice.* Research Results of the Scientific Network PhiMSAMP (pp. 1–24). London, College Publications.

Gelfert, A. (2022). Thinking with notations: Epistemic actions and epistemic activities in mathematical practice. In Friedman, M., & Krauthausen, K. (eds.), *Model and Mathematics: From the 19th to the 21st Century: Trends in the History of Science* (pp. 333–62). Cham, Birkhäuser.

Goethe, N. B., & Friend, M. (2010). Confronting ideals of proof with the ways of proving of the research mathematician. *Studia Logica,* 96(2), 273–88.

Gonthier, G. (2008). Formal proof – The four-color theorem. *Notices of the American Mathematical Society,* 55(11), 1382–93.

Greco, J. (2010). *Achieving Knowledge.* Cambridge, Cambridge University Press.

Greiffenhagen, C., & Sharrock, W. (2005). Gestures in the blackboard work of mathematics instruction. Paper presented at Interacting Bodies: Proceedings of 2nd Conference of the International Society for Gesture Studies (Lyon, 15–18 June 2005), pp. 1–24. http://gesture-lyon2005.ens-lyon.fr/IMG/pdf/Greiffenhagen-Gesture.pdf.

Habgood-Coote, J., & Tanswell, F. S. (2023). Group knowledge and mathematical collaboration: A philosophical examination of the classification of finite simple groups. *Episteme*, 20(2), 281–307.

Haffner, E. (2021). The shaping of Dedekind's rigorous mathematics: What do Dedekind's drafts tell us about his ideal of rigor? *Notre Dame Journal of Formal Logic*, 62(1), 5–31.

Hales, T. C. (2008). Formal proof. *Notices of the AMS*, 55(11), 1370–80.

Hamami, Y. (2019). Mathematical rigor and proof. *Review of Symbolic Logic*, 15(2), 409–49.

Hamami, Y., & Morris, R. L. (2020). Philosophy of mathematical practice: A primer for mathematics educators. *ZDM*, 52(6), 1113–26.

Hanna, G., & Larvor, B. (2020). As Thurston says? On using quotations from famous mathematicians to make points about philosophy and education. *ZDM: Mathematics Education*, 52(6), 1137–47.

Hardy, G. H. (1929). Mathematical proof. *Mind*, 38(149), 1–25.

Hegel, G. W. F. (1807). *Phenomenology of Spirit*. Miller, A. V. (trans.), 1977. Oxford, Clarendon Press.

Heinze, A. (2010). Mathematicians' individual criteria for accepting theorems and proofs: An empirical approach. In Hanna, G., Jahnke, H. N., & Pulte, H. (eds.), *Explanation and Proof in Mathematics* (pp. 101–11). Boston, MA, Springer.

Hengel, E. (2022). Publishing while female: Are women held to higher standards? Evidence from peer review. *The Economic Journal*, 132(648), 2951–91. https://doi.org/10.1093/ej/ueac032.

Hersh, R. (1993). Proving is convincing and explaining. *Educational Studies in Mathematics*, 24(4), 389–99.

Hersh, R. (1997). Prove – Once more and again. *Philosophia Mathematica (III)*, 5(2), 153–65.

Hilbert, D. (1899). *Grundlagen der Geometrie*. Leipzig, Teubner.

Hookway, C. (2010). Some varieties of epistemic injustice: Reflections on Fricker. *Episteme*, 7(2), 151–63.

Hornsby, J. (2012). Ryle's knowing-how, and knowing how to act. In Bengson, J., & Moffett, M. A. (eds.), *Knowing How: Essays on Knowledge, Mind and Action* (pp. 80–98). Oxford, Oxford University Press.

Hunsicker, E., & Rittberg, C. J. (2022). On the epistemological relevance of social power and justice in mathematics. *Axiomathes*, 32, 1147–68.

Hursthouse, R., & Pettigrove, G. (2022). Virtue ethics. In Zalta, E. N., & Nodelman, U. (eds.), *Stanford Encyclopedia of Philosophy* (Winter 2022 Edition). https://plato.stanford.edu/archives/win2022/entries/ethics-virtue/.

Inglis, M., & Aberdein, A. (2015). Beauty is not simplicity: An analysis of mathematicians' proof appraisals. *Philosophia Mathematica (III)*, 23(1), 87–109.

Inglis, M., & Aberdein, A. (2016). Diversity in proof appraisal. In Larvor, B. (ed.), *Mathematical Cultures* (pp. 163–79. Cham, Birkhäuser.

Inglis, M., & Alcock, L. (2012). Expert and novice approaches to reading mathematical proofs. *Journal for Research in Mathematics Education*, 43(4), 358–90.

Inglis, M., Mejía-Ramos, J. P., Weber, K., & Alcock, L. (2013). On mathematicians' different standards when evaluating elementary proofs. *Topics in Cognitive Science*, 5(2), 270–82.

Isaacson, D. (2011). The reality of mathematics and the case of set theory. In Noviak, Z. & Simonyi, A. (eds.), *Truth, Reference, and Realism* (pp. 1–75). Budapest, Central European University Press.

Jaffe, A., & Quinn, F. (1993). 'Theoretical mathematics': Toward a cultural synthesis of mathematics and theoretical physics. *Bulletin of the American Mathematical Society*, 29(1), 1–13.

Kirsh, D., & Maglio, P. (1994). On distinguishing epistemic from pragmatic action. *Cognitive Science*, 18(4), 513–49.

Kitcher, P. (1984). *The Nature of Mathematical Knowledge*. Oxford, Oxford University Press.

Kneebone, G. T. (1957). The philosophical basis of mathematical rigour. *Philosophical Quarterly*, 7(28), 204–23.

Knipping, C., & Reid, D. A. (2019). Argumentation analysis for early career researchers. In Kaiser, G. & Presmeg, N. (eds.), *Compendium for Early Career Researchers in Mathematics Education* (pp. 3–31). Cham, Springer.

Kreisel, G. (1967). Informal rigour and completeness proofs. In Lakatos, I. (ed.), *Studies in Logic and the Foundations of Mathematics*, Vol. 47 (pp. 138–86). Amsterdam, Elsevier.

Kunen, K. (1980). *Set Theory: An Introduction to Independence Proofs*. Amsterdam, North-Holland.

Kurji, A. H. (2021). *What the Heck Is Logic? Logics-as-Formalizations, a Nihilistic Approach*. Doctoral dissertation, University of Bristol. https://research-information.bris.ac.uk/en/studentTheses/what-the-heck-is-logic.

Lakatos, I. (1976). *Proofs and Refutations: The Logic of Mathematical Discovery*. Cambridge, Cambridge University Press.

Lane, L., Martin, U., Murray-Rust, D., Pease, A., & Tanswell, F. (2019). Journeys in mathematical landscapes: Genius or craft? In Hanna, G., Reid, D. A., & de Villiers, M. (eds.), *Proof Technology in Mathematics Research and Teaching* (pp. 197–212). Cham, Springer.

Larvor, B. (2001). What is dialectical philosophy of mathematics? *Philosophia Mathematica (III)*, 9, 212–29.

Larvor, B. (2012). How to think about informal proofs. *Synthese*, 187(2), 715–30.

Larvor, B. (2016). Why the naïve derivation recipe model cannot explain how mathematicians' proofs secure mathematical knowledge. *Philosophia Mathematica (III)*, 24(3), 401–4.

Leitgeb, H. (2009). On formal and informal provability. In Bueno, O., & Linnebo, Ø. (eds.), *New Waves in Philosophy of Mathematics* (pp. 263–99). London, Palgrave Macmillan.

Lob, H., & Richmond, H. W. (1930). On the solutions of Malfatti's problem for a triangle. *Proceedings of the London Mathematical Society*, 2(1), 287–304.

Lombardi, G. (2022a). Proving the solution of Malfatti's marble problem. *Rendiconti del Circolo Matematico di Palermo*, Series 72, 1751–82. https://doi.org/10.1007/s12215-022-00759-2.

Lombardi, G. (2022b). Demistifying Malfatti's marble problem. *Medium*, 27 June. https://medium.com/@giancarlolombardi_25894/demistifying-malfattis-marble-problem-fcb0a4b98b36.

Löwe, B. (2016). Philosophy or not? The study of cultures and practices of mathematics. In Ju, S., Löwe, B., Müller, T., & Xie, Y. (eds.), *Cultures of Mathematics and Logic* (pp. 23–42). Cham, Birkhäuser.

Löwe, B., & Müller, T. (2008). Mathematical knowledge is context-dependent. *Grazer Philosophische Studien*, 76, 91–107.

Löwe, B., & Müller, T. (2010). Skills and mathematical knowledge. In Löwe, B., & Müller, T. (eds.), *Philosophy of Mathematics: Sociological Aspects and Mathematical Practice* (pp. 265–80). London, College Publications.

Löwe, B., & Müller, T. (2011). Data and phenomena in conceptual modelling. *Synthese*, 182(1), 131–48.

Löwe, B., & Van Kerkhove, B. (2019). Methodological triangulation in empirical philosophy (of mathematics). In Aberdein, A., & Inglis, M. (eds.), *Advances in Experimental Philosophy of Logic and Mathematics* (pp. 15–37). New York, Bloomsbury Academic Publishers.

Mac Lane, S. (1986). *Mathematics: Form and Function*. New York, Springer-Verlag.

MacIntyre, A. (1985). *After Virtue*, 2nd Edition. London, Duckworth.

MacKenzie, D. (2004). *Mechanizing Proof: Computing, Risk, and Trust*. London, MIT Press.

Maddy, P. (2017). Set-theoretic foundations. In Caicedo, A., Cummings, J., Koellner, P., & Larson, P. B. (eds.), *Contemporary Mathematics 690:*

Foundations of Mathematics (pp. 289–322). Providence, RI, American Mathematical Society.

Maddy, P. (2019). What do we want a foundation to do? Comparing set-theoretic, category-theoretic, and univalent approaches. In Centrone, S., Kant, D., & Sarikaya, D. (eds), *Reflections on the Foundations of Mathematics: Univalent Foundations, Set Theory and General Thoughts* (pp. 293–311). Cham, Springer.

Malfatti, G. (1803). Memoria sopra un problema sterotomico. *Memorie di matematica e di fisica della Societá Italiana delle Scienze*, 10(1), 235–44.

Martin, J. V. (2021). Prolegomena to virtue-theoretic studies in the philosophy of mathematics. *Synthese*, 199(1), 1409–34.

Maxwell, E. A. (1959). *Fallacies in Mathematics*. Cambridge, Cambridge University Press.

Mejía-Ramos, J. P., & Weber, K. (2014). Why and how mathematicians read proofs: Further evidence from a survey study. *Educational Studies in Mathematics*, 85(2), 161–73.

Mihaljević, H., & Santamaría, L. (2022). Mathematics publications and authors' gender: Learning from the Gender Gap in Science project. *European Mathematical Society Magazine*, 123, 34–8.

Mihaljević, H., Santamaría, L., & Tullney, M. (2016). The effect of gender in the publication patterns in mathematics. *PLoS One*, 11(10), e0165367. https://doi.org/10.1371/journal.pone.0165367.

Montmarquet, J. (1993). *Epistemic Virtue and Doxastic Responsibility*. Lanham, MD, Rowman & Littlefield.

Moore, R. C. (2016). Mathematics professors' evaluation of students' proofs: A complex teaching practice. *International Journal of Research in Undergraduate Mathematics Education*, 2(2), 246–78.

Morris, R. L. (2021). Intellectual generosity and the reward structure of mathematics. *Synthese*, 199(1), 345–67.

Müller-Hill, E. (2009). Formalizability and knowledge ascriptions in mathematical practice. *Philosophia Scientiæ: Travaux d'histoire et de philosophie des sciences*, 13(2), 21–43.

Müller-Hill, E. (2011). *Die epistemische Rolle formalisierbarer mathematischer Beweise*. Doctoral dissertation, University of Bonn. https://bonndoc .ulb.uni-bonn.de/xmlui/handle/20.500.11811/4850.

Mumma, J. (2010). Proofs, pictures, and Euclid. *Synthese*, 175(2), 255–87.

Nelsen, R. B. (1993). *Proofs without Words: Exercises in Visual Thinking*. Washington, DC, Mathematical Association of America.

Nelson, R. B. (2000). *Proofs without Words II: More Exercises in Visual Thinking*. Washington, DC, Mathematical Association of America.

Nelsen, R. B. (2008). Visual gems of number theory. *Math Horizons*, 15(3), 7–31.

Nelsen, R. B. (2015). *Proofs without Words III: Further Exercises in Visual Thinking*. Washington, DC, Mathematical Association of America.

Ohlhorst, J. (2022). Dual processes, dual virtues. *Philosophical Studies*, 179(7), 2237–57.

Ording, P. (2019). *99 Variations on a Proof*. Princeton, NJ, Princeton University Press.

Panse, A., Alcock, L., & Inglis, M. (2018). Reading proofs for validation and comprehension: An expert–novice eye-movement study. *International Journal of Research in Undergraduate Mathematics Education*, 4(3), 357–75.

Pelc, A. (2009). Why do we believe theorems? *Philosophia Mathematica (III)*, 17(1), 84–94.

Pettigrew, R. (2016). Review of John P. Burgess's *Rigor and Structure*. *Philosophia Mathematica (III)*, 24, 129–46.

Popper, K. (1959) *The Logic of Scientific Discovery*. London, Hutchinson. (First published in German as *Logik der Forschung*, 1934.)

Popper, K. (1963) *Conjectures and Refutations: The Growth of Scientific Knowledge*. London, Routledge & Kegan Paul.

Priest, G. (1987). *In Contradiction: A Study of the Transconsistent*. Oxford, Oxford University Press.

Rav, Y. (1999). Why do we prove theorems? *Philosophia Mathematica (III)*, 7(1), 5–41.

Rittberg, C. J. (2021). Intellectual humility in mathematics. *Synthese*, 199(3), 5571–601.

Rittberg, C. J. (2023). Justified epistemic exclusion in mathematics. *Philosophia Mathematica (III)*, 31(3), 330–59,

Rittberg, C. J., Tanswell, F. S., & Van Bendegem, J. P. (2020). Epistemic injustice in mathematics. *Synthese*, 197(9), 3875–3904.

Rodin, A. (2014). On constructive axiomatic method. arXiv preprint, arXiv:1408.3591. https://arxiv.org/abs/1408.3591.

Rolfsen, D. (1976). *Knots and Links*. Berkeley, CA: Publish or Perish.

Rotman, B. (1988). Towards a semiotics of mathematics. *Semiotica*, 72, 1–35.

Ruffino, M., San Mauro, L., & Venturi, G. (2021). Speech acts in mathematics. *Synthese*, 198(10), 10063–87.

Russell, G. (2018). Logical nihilism: Could there be no logic? *Philosophical Issues*, 28(1), 308–24.

Russell, G. (2019). Logical pluralism. In Zalta, E. N. (ed.), *Stanford Encyclopedia of Philosophy*. https://plato.stanford.edu/entries/logical-pluralism/.

Ryle, G. (1946). Knowing how and knowing that: The presidential address. *Proceedings of the Aristotelian Society*, 46, 1–16.

Ryle, G. (1971). Thinking and self-teaching. *Journal of Philosophy of Education*, 5, 216–28.

Sangwin, C. (2023). Sums of the first n odd integers. *Mathematical Gazette*, 107(568), 10–24.

Sangwin, C. J., & Kinnear, G. (2021). Investigating insight and rigour as separate constructs in mathematical proof. EdarXiv preprint. https://doi.org/10.35542/osf.io/egks4.

Sangwin, C., & Tanswell, F. S. (2023). Developing new picture proofs that the sums of the first n odd integers are squares. *Mathematical Gazette*, 107(569), 249–62.

Schlimm, D. 2012. Mathematical concepts and investigative practice. In Feest, U. & Steinle, F. (eds.), *Scientific Concepts and Investigative Practice* (pp. 127–47). Berlin, de Gruyter GmbH.

Secco, G. D., & Pereira, L. C. (2017). Proofs versus experiments: Wittgensteinian themes surrounding the four-color theorem. In Silva, M. (ed.), *How Colours Matter to Philosophy* (pp. 289–307). Cham, Springer.

Shapiro, S. (2014). *Varieties of Logic*. Oxford, Oxford University Press.

Shapiro, S., & Roberts, C. (2021). Open texture and mathematics. *Notre Dame Journal of Formal Logic*, 62(1), 173–91.

Shin, S. J. (1994). *The Logical Status of Diagrams*. Cambridge, Cambridge University Press.

Sosa, E. (2009). Knowing full well: The normativity of beliefs as performances. *Philosophical Studies*, 142(1), 5–15.

Steiner, J. (1826). Einige geometrische Betrachtungen. *Journal für die reine und angewandte Mathematik*, 1826 (1), 161–84. https://doi.org/10.1515/crll.1826.1.161. Reprinted as Steiner, J. (1901) in Stern, R. (ed.), *Einige geometrische Betrachtungen* (section 14, pp. 25–7). Leipzig: Verlag von Wilhelm Engelmann. https://archive.org/details/einigegeometris01steigoog/page/n29/mode/2up?view=theater.

Steiner, M. (1975). *Mathematical Knowledge*. Ithaca, NY, Cornell University Press.

Su, F. (2017). Mathematics for human flourishing. *American Mathematical Monthly*, 124(6), 483–93.

Su, F. (2020). *Mathematics for Human Flourishing*. New Haven, CT, Yale University Press.

Tanswell, F. (2015). A problem with the dependence of informal proofs on formal proofs. *Philosophia Mathematica (III)*, 23(3), 295–310.

Tanswell, F. S. (2016a). Saving proof from paradox: Gödel's paradox and the inconsistency of informal mathematics. In Andreas, H., & Verdée, P. (eds.), *Logical Studies of Paraconsistent Reasoning in Science and Mathematics* (pp. 159–73). Cham, Springer.

Tanswell, F. S. (2016b). *Proof, Rigour and Informality: A Virtue Account of Mathematical Knowledge.* Doctoral dissertation, University of St Andrews. https://research-repository.st-andrews.ac.uk/handle/10023/10249.

Tanswell, F. (2017). Playing with LEGO® and proving theorems. In Cook, R. T., & Bacharach, S. (eds.), *LEGO® and Philosophy: Constructing Reality Brick by Brick* (pp. 217–26). Hoboken, NJ, Wiley Blackwell.

Tanswell, F. S. (2018). Conceptual engineering for mathematical concepts. *Inquiry*, 61(8), 881–913.

Tanswell, F. S. (in press). Go forth and multiply! On actions, instructions and imperatives in mathematical proofs. In Bueno, O., & Brown, J. (eds.), *Essays on the Philosophy of Jody Azzouni.* Cham, Springer.

Tanswell, F. S., & Inglis, M. (2023) The language of proofs: A philosophical corpus linguistics study of instructions and imperatives in mathematical texts. In Sriraman, B. (ed.), *Handbook of the History and Philosophy of Mathematical Practice* (pp. 1–30). Cham, Springer. https://link.springer.com/referenceworkentry/10.1007/978-3-030-19071-2_50-1.

Tanswell, F. S., & Kidd, I. J. (2021). Mathematical practice and epistemic virtue and vice. *Synthese*, 199(1), 407–26.

Tanswell, F. S., & Rittberg, C. J. (2020). Epistemic injustice in mathematics education. *ZDM: Mathematics Education*, 52(6), 1199–1210.

Tappenden, J. (2008). Mathematical concepts and definitions. In Mancosu, P. (ed.), *The Philosophy of Mathematical Practice* (pp. 256–75). Oxford, Oxford University Press.

Tatton-Brown, O. (2021). Rigour and intuition. *Erkenntnis*, 86, 1757–81.

Tatton-Brown, O. (2023). Rigour and proof. *Review of Symbolic Logic*, 16(2), 480–508.

Termini, M. (2019). Proving the point: Connections between legal and mathematical reasoning. *Suffolk University Law Review*, 52, 5–35.

Thomas, R. S. D. (2007). The comparison of mathematics with narrative. In Van Kerkhove, B., & Van Bendegem, J. P. (eds.), *Perspectives on Mathematical Practices* (pp. 43–59). Dordrecht, Springer.

Thomas, R. S. D. (2015). The judicial analogy for mathematical publication. In Zack, M., & Landry, E. (eds.), *Research in History and Philosophy of Mathematics* (pp. 161–70. Cham, Birkhäuser.

Thomas, R. S. D. (2017). Beauty is not all there is to aesthetics in mathematics. *Philosophia Mathematica (III)*, 25(1), 116–27.

Thompson, C. J. (1986). The contributions of Mark Kac to mathematical physics. *Annals of Probability*, 14(4), 1129–38.

Thurston, W. P. (1994). On proof and progress in mathematics. *Bulletin of the American Mathematical Society*, 30(2), 161–77.

Toulmin, S. E. (1958). *The Uses of Argument*. Cambridge, Cambridge University Press.

Toulmin, S., Rieke, R., & Janik, A. (1979). *An Introduction to Reasoning*. London, Macmillan.

Van Bendegem, J. P. (2014). The impact of the philosophy of mathematical practice on the philosophy of mathematics. In Soler, L., Zwart, S., Lynch, M., & Israel-Jost, V. (eds.), *Science After the Practice Turn in the Philosophy, History, and Social Studies of Science* (pp. 215–26). Abingdon, UK, Taylor & Francis.

Vecht, J. J. (2023). Open texture clarified. *Inquiry*, 66(6), 1120–40.

Vučković, A., & Sikimić, V. (2023). How to fight linguistic injustice in science: Equity measures and mitigating agents. *Social Epistemology*, 37(1), 80–96.

Waismann, F. (1968). Verifiability. In Flew, A. (ed.), *Logic and Language* (pp. 118–44). Oxford, Basil Blackwell.

Walton, D. N. (1998). *The New Dialectic: Conversational Contexts of Argument*. Toronto, University of Toronto Press.

Walton, D., & Krabbe, E. C. (1995). *Commitment in Dialogue: Basic Concepts of Interpersonal Reasoning*. Albany, NY, State University of New York Press.

Weber, K. (2008). How mathematicians determine if an argument is a valid proof. *Journal for Research in Mathematics Education*, 39(4), 431–59.

Weber, K. (2023). Instructions and constructions in set theory proofs. *Synthese*, 202(2), 1–17.

Weber, K., & Czocher, J. (2019). On mathematicians' disagreements on what constitutes a proof. *Research in Mathematics Education*, 21(3), 251–70.

Weber, K., & Tanswell, F. S. (2022). Instructions and recipes in mathematical proofs. *Educational Studies in Mathematics*, 11(1), 73–87.

Weber, K., Mejía-Ramos, J. P., & Volpe, T. (2022). The relationship between proof and certainty in mathematical practice. *Journal for Research in Mathematics Education*, 53(1), 65–84.

Weir, A. (2016). Informal proof, formal proof, formalism. *Review of Symbolic Logic*, 9(1), 23–43.

Weisgerber, S. (2022). Visual proofs as counterexamples to the standard view of informal mathematical proofs? In Giardino, V., Linker, S., Burns, R., et al. (eds.), *Diagrammatic Representation and Inference*. 13th International Conference, Diagrams 2022, Rome, 14–16 September. Lecture Notes in

Computer Science, vol. 13462. Cham, Springer. https://doi.org/10.1007/978-3-031-15146-0_3.

Whitehead, A. N., & Russell, B. (1910). *Principia Mathematica, Volume I.* Cambridge, Cambridge University Press.

Wiedijk, F. (2008). Formal proof – Getting started. *Notices of the American Mathematical Society*, 55(11), 1408–14.

Zagzebski, L. T. (1996). *Virtues of the Mind*. Cambridge, Cambridge University Press.

Zalgaller, V. A., & Los', G. A. (1994). The solution of Malfatti's problem. *Journal of Mathematical Sciences*, 72(4), 3163–77.

Zayton, B. (2022). Open texture, rigor, and proof. *Synthese*, 200(4), 1–20.

Zeilberger, D. (1993). Theorems for a price: Tomorrow's semi-rigorous mathematical culture. *Notices of the American Mathematical Society*, 40, 978–81.

Acknowledgements

Many thanks to all the friends and colleagues who have provided encouragement or feedback on this Element: Andrew Aberdein, Lara Alcock, Neil Barton, Ben Davies, Silvia De Toffoli, Catarina Dutilh Novaes, Axel Gelfert, Paola Iannone, Matthew Inglis, Aadil Kurji, Brendan Larvor, Benedikt Löwe, Ursula Martin, Ásgeir Berg Matthíasson, Darren O'Byrne, Colin Rittberg, Chris Sangwin, Joe Slater, Keith Weber, Arlette Zunneberg, and an anonymous referee. Thanks also to audiences in Bochum, organised by Hitoshi Omori, and of the online *Formalize!(?)* conference, organised by Deniz Sarikaya.

Much of the writing of this *Element* was funded by the Research Foundation – Flanders (FWO) Project G083620N: "The Epistemology of Data Science: Mathematics and the Critical Research Agenda on Data Practices". My thanks to Karen Francois and Patrick Allo for their support.

Thanks to Roger Nelsen, Dale Rolfsen, the AMS, and Andrew Aberdein for help and permissions to use their respective images.

Finally, thanks to everyone who made it possible to work on this Element by helping with childcare and familial support: mum & Chris, Thecla, Angela, Michael & Petra, dad & Sarah, and everyone at my son's Kita. Most importantly, love and thanks to Lea and Ingmar.

Cambridge Elements ≡

The Philosophy of Mathematics

Penelope Rush
University of Tasmania
From the time Penny Rush completed her thesis in the philosophy of mathematics (2005), she has worked continuously on themes around the realism/anti-realism divide and the nature of mathematics. Her edited collection, *The Metaphysics of Logic* (Cambridge University Press, 2014), and forthcoming essay 'Metaphysical Optimism' (*Philosophy Supplement*), highlight a particular interest in the idea of reality itself and curiosity and respect as important philosophical methodologies.

Stewart Shapiro
The Ohio State University
Stewart Shapiro is the O'Donnell Professor of Philosophy at The Ohio State University, a Distinguished Visiting Professor at the University of Connecticut, and a Professorial Fellow at the University of Oslo. His major works include *Foundations without Foundationalism* (1991), *Philosophy of Mathematics: Structure and Ontology* (1997), *Vagueness in Context* (2006), and *Varieties of Logic* (2014). He has taught courses in logic, philosophy of mathematics, metaphysics, epistemology, philosophy of religion, Jewish philosophy, social and political philosophy, and medical ethics.

About the Series

This Cambridge Elements series provides an extensive overview of the philosophy of mathematics in its many and varied forms. Distinguished authors will provide an up-to-date summary of the results of current research in their fields and give their own take on what they believe are the most significant debates influencing research, drawing original conclusions.

Cambridge Elements ≡

The Philosophy of Mathematics

Printed in the United States
by Baker & Taylor Publisher Services